'And near Killala is a ruin, in very good preservation,
called Baal-Tien, The House of Baal'

Drawing and description by Miss L.C. Beaufort, 1825.

MORRIGAN
an imprint of
Morigna MediaCo Teo
Killala
County Mayo

© Conan Kennedy, 1994, 1997

ISBN 0 907677 96 7

Cover by Penhouse, Dublin.

Origination by Morigna MediaCo Teo
Printed by ColourBooks Ltd., Dublin.

Conan Kennedy
is also author of
(with Daragh Smith)

Places of Mythology

MORRIGAN BOOKS

ANCIENT IRELAND
THE USER'S GUIDE

An Exploration of Ireland's
Pre-Christian Monuments,
Mythology and Magic,
Ritual and Folklore

CONAN KENNEDY

The book is in three sections. These deal separately with
Ancient Monuments and Artifacts, with Mythology,
and with the folklore of Ritual and Magic.
The general introduction starts on page 5,

Part One –Monuments and Artifacts, begins on page 8

Part Two – Irish Mythology, begins on page 29

Part Three – Magic Ritual & Religion, begins on page 61

The Index starts on page 106
A Mini Bibliography is on page 112

The illustrations on the front cover are
(from right to left)
Stone idol from Beltany, Co. Donegal;
Part of stone alignment at Gurranes, Co. Cork; triple spiral at Newgrange.

AT THE START OF IT ALL . . .

FLINT WIELDING CHARACTERS wandered around Ireland ten thousand years ago. This period is defined by archaeologists as the Old Stone Age, 8000 - 7000BC. Little evidence of these early inhabitants remains, and little is known of them. It is generally said that they 'came from' Scotland or Western Britain, but this may only be because to Irish academics everything 'comes from' somewhere else. Then, within Ireland, this thought continues, things newly arrived change and, by some unexplained process, they become 'Irish'. What precisely defines this Irishness is not explained either. Concepts such as tribal consciousness and the interplay between that and the spirits of the land have been avoided. Such concepts are politically incorrect. Dangerous racial and nationalistic tensions lurk beneath the surface of the Irish psyche . . .the veneer of euro-thought must be maintained lest these tensions explode into chaos. This is why the nature of Ireland, both ancient and modern, remains so obscure and mysterious. Our understanding has been hampered by fear of what we may discover. We are in the position of trying to explain the motor car, while denying the existence of wheels!

But back to way back then. No doubt then, ten thousand years ago, life was lived in a form of quiet chaos. Quiet because there were really far too few people around to make for lively wars and cultural clashes. Though after about five thousand years things began to look up. New guys 'came from' Britain and continental Europe, new guys with the then new fangled polished stone axes. Not exactly the cutting edge of technology by our terms, but technology with sufficient cutting edge to cut down forests and get things going in agriculture.

They grew wheat and barley. And they kept sheep, and goats, and cattle. They lived in little groups, in huts. These huts, this making of their own space, this was the essential difference between them and their predecessors. The earlier flint wielding people were no doubt more in tune with nature, being part of nature themselves. But the new polished stone folks were coming to be in tune with themselves. The concept of their humanity grew in them, and they started to see their soul. And they became aware of the spirit.

So they built huge tombs.

Megalithic. Big stones. Really big stones! While the reasons for such particular tombs are looked at later under the appropriate heading of 'stones', the facts and locations of megalithic monuments are dealt with in part one of the book. These tombs are, in fact, very different and fall into fairly definable classifications. In big-stone-speak we are talking of the period around 4000 - 2000BC. Conventional archaeological thinking has it that during this period 'waves' of new cultures arrived in Ireland, bringing with them new styles of tombs. Perhaps. But we must remember also that cultures change through internal dynamics. And ideas travel independently of mass migrations. A few hundred years after Christ there were Christian Holy Men on remote islands off the west coast of Ireland. It is a long way from Jerusalem to Inishkea. But new has always travelled fast. Bad news is notoriously speedy, but faster still is news of hope, and the possibility of eternal life. . . salvation!

Hope, and the possibility of eternal life inspired our ancestors to build their great stone tombs. Magnificent structures, particularly compared to the huts in which they spent their lives. Different priorities in those days. Our modern goal is to live in a nice house and OK, to hell with it if down the road there are neglected graveyards full of degenerate vandals. We don't care. That's death down there, nothing in that for us.

In ancient Ireland it was different. There was nothing much in life for anyone, nothing of a material nature. But there were frequent glimpses, even visions, of the beyond, the spirit world. Magic was common-place. And the driving force of life was to move into that 'beyond', that spirit world, to be at one with the mystery. Though they probably didn't phrase it quite like that.

Then along came the Bronze Age. From about 2000BC - 500BC this new metal was the thing. Other metals too. Gold. And the working of copper, apart from its use in bronze, was widespread. New ideas and technologies blossomed. Big stone structures became out of fashion. Except for big stone circles, many of which in Ireland are felt to date from this period. These circles were for ritual, no doubt unpleasant to our modern minds, and perhaps also for quasi-astronomical observation, certainly inaccurate to our modern methods. The Bronze Age folks also erected standing stones, though it's not easy to tell the dates of these. Frankly it's not easy to tell the dates of anything to do with big stones, a thousand year margin of error is quite acceptable to archaeologists. Like that of economics, this is one of those professions which is always proved wrong by the next generation.

Goodbye to the great days of great stones then around 1000BC. And then sometime about 500BC came iron. Now we're talking modern times. The Iron Age peoples were just like us. They built houses and habitations and we know all about them, what they ate, what they did in the afternoon and so forth, except we know little or nothing about their burial customs or tombs. Perhaps they were too busy with their other constructions, such as hill forts and stone and earthen raths. These very numerous Iron Age structures merge with those of the early historical period, a time which itself brings the first hints of Christianity. And at the first hint of Christianity, this book stops. Not for religious reasons, and certainly not because it is a clean cut-off point where things changed completely straight away. Far from it, things changed very gradually. Christianity took a very long time to get below the surface. And how far below the surface it did ever get is hard to judge. On the very day this introduction is being written, there appears in the newspapers a report. A donkey has been found slaughtered on Dublin's Howth Head. Police say it appears to have been a 'seasonal ritual'!

Beneath the surface, what lies beneath the surface? One thing that rests, though 'rests' is not the right word, one thing that bubbles there is certainly the story. Made up of history, and of lies and hopes and poetry in various measure, the story weaves this way and that and changes. It changes only to reappear hundreds of years later, thousands of years later. And when it re-appears we see that it is still the way it was before it changed, we thought, forever. The heart of the story is what we call myth, mythology. But whatever it is, and whatever it is called, it is not easy to grasp or understand. It exists in what the aboriginal Australians call 'dreamtime', a concept itself difficult to understand.

A fashionable international historian has written in recent years that we are at 'the end of history'. Whatever, it is also fashionable to suppose that we are at the end of mythology, that such things belong to the past, and that there they lie, fossils. To be studied, categorised, numbered in university departments. Researchers roam remote regions recording old stories from old people. Valuable, no doubt, but perhaps more revealing would be research into the young people who slaughter donkies in seasonal rituals. Few investigate them, other. than moronic tabloid reporters, hopeful that there may be naked women involved. People who can think are afraid to think. Perhaps they are right. Perhaps, waiting to be born, as the poet said, there really is a beast. We cannot really know, though many have suspicions.

One certainty among the doubts and suspicions. Somewhere in Ancient Ireland the truth is hidden. Whether that truth be one of beast, or of beauty, of darkness, or of light... a foolish modern question!

Disc in bronze, La Tene period, National Museum, Dublin.

7

PART ONE

MONUMENTS
and
ARTIFACTS

Ogham Stone at Breastagh, near Killala, Co.Mayo

'Monuments' is an archaeological term for structures left on the land-scape by earlier civilizations. 'Artifacts' is a word used to describe moveable objects created by such civilizations. The essential differ-ence used to be that 'monuments' are usually too big to move. Though, in this age of the JCB, in 1992 as these words are written, it is reported that a large megalithic tomb has been moved to the forecourt of a hotel in County Louth!

Artifacts have always been moved about. Decorated stones and such-like have been carried away to new sites at the whim of landowners. Objects found in the field have invariably been whisked away to museums or private collections. In pre-Independence the British Museum was the ultimate destination of many items, and since then the National Museum in Dublin has been their last resting place. Until very recently very few artifacts have been on view in their locality of discovery. Nowadays there are several small local displays, some-times with items on loan from larger collections elsewhere.

FIELD MONUMENTS

Megalithic Tombs

Built of large stones, these consist of a burial chamber or chambers, constructed with large uprights and roofed over in stone. These were originally contained within a cairn (heap of stones) or an earthen mound, with access through an entrance. In most cases the covering cairn or mound is gone, leaving only the large stones. These structures are commonly called Dolmens, Cromlechs or 'Druids Altars'. Archaeologists divide them into the four classifications on pages 10 and 11 overleaf.

Drumanone Dolmen, near Boyle, County Roscommon

Types of megalithic tombs:

Court Tombs
date from before 3000 BC. They are so called because of the open court at the entrance to the tomb. This was used for religious ceremonies. Court tombs generally are aligned to face east. Burials were cremated and grave goods such as pots and arrowheads were placed with the ashes of the interred.

Below left, Ground plan of Court tomb at Creevykeel, Co Sligo.
Below right, Distribution of Court Tombs.

Portal Tombs
are a simple form of gallery-tomb consisting of at least three upright stones bearing one or more capstones. These are the characteristic 'dolmens' of which there are around 150 in Ireland. They generally date from the years 2500 to 2000 BC.

Below left, Ground plans of portal tombs at Proleek, Co.Louth and (bottom left) Kilfeaghan, Co.Down. Uprights shown black, capstone outlined.
Below right, Distribution of Court Tombs.

Passage Tombs

consist essentially of a round mound or cairn with a passage leading from the edge to a chamber within. Along with the Portal and Court tombs they belong to the Neolithic age (c4000-200 BC). Newgrange is a characteristic example of a passage tomb; many were faced with white quartz and generally they are found in concentrations. Around 300 survive.

Below left, Carrowkeel, Co.Sligo, Passage Tomb. Plan of Chamber (top left), Section through mound showing extent of passage.
Below right, distribution of Passage Tombs.

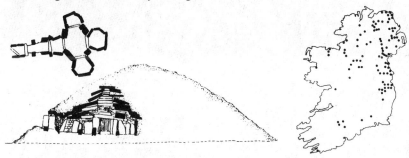

Wedge Tombs

belong to the Early Bronze Age (after 2000 BC); consisting of a chamber that often narrows and lowers towards the back. The entrances-generally face the winter setting sun. There are around 400 surviving (with over 100 in Co.Clare's Burren area). It is felt these wedge tombs were built by the first Celtic- speaking peoples coming from France.

Below left, Ground plan of Wedge Tomb at Island, Co.Cork. (Dotted line shows original extent of cairn).
Below right, distribution of Wedge Tombs.

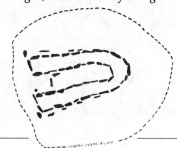

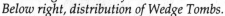

Two of Ireland's major sites are (above) The Grianan of Aileach,in County Donegal and (below) Medb's Cairn at Knocknarea, Co.Sligo.

FIELD MONUMENTS *(Continued)*

Mounds, Cairns And Barrows

Circular mounds or cairns of rounded profile and various size are found widely. Generally burial-mounds, they may cover many different types of burial from different eras. In addition to some of those listed on previous pages, burials in mounds may be in cists. These were stone boxes made of slabs, of Neolithic origin, the burials being accompanied by pottery. Bronze Age Cist burials are also found under round mounds, these usually smaller than the Neolithic. Ringbarrows are low mounds with encircling ditch and bank, diameter from 4 to 20 metres. These can occur in clusters and are generally of Bronze or Iron Age date.

Ringforts

By far the most numerous monument on the landscape, an estimated 30 to 40 thousand of these structures have been identified. Their construction ranges over the whole period from Neolithic to Mediaeval date. Ringforts comprise a circular area of usually around 25m to 50m in diameter surrounded by an earthen bank thrown up from a ditch immediately outside. Some are oval or D-shaped, some have more than one bank or ditch. These ringforts are the 'raths' so common in Irish placenames.

Stone Forts

In some areas the bank is replaced by a massive stone wall. These types of ringfort are called a caher, cashel or stone fort and well-preserved examples may have terraces and steps in the inner face of the wall. The majority, however, are only traces of stone in a circular pattern, the walls having been taken away for later purposes.

Hillforts And Promontory Forts

Some early forts were constructed so as to take maximum advantage of natural features such as low hills and promontories. These structures are generally assigned to the Iron Age, consisting of banks and ditches enclosing either the top of a hill or cutting off a headland or promontory. In some cases these banks were replaced by massive stone walls and defensive works.

Stone Circles

Numbering around 180, stone circles are found in two main groups, Mid-Ulster and Cork-Kerry. There are a small number in Dublin-Wicklow and Lough Gur and a few elsewhere. The Cork-Kerry circles tend to be the most physically impressive, ranging from 4 to 17 metres in diameter with up to seventeen stones. Circles are found in combination with alignments and burials and would be contemporaneous with Wedge tombs, *(see previous pages).* Functions of circles is obscure, but on balance would appear to be for ritual purposes. Theories concerning astronomical observations are generally discredited. The Cork-Kerry circles are generally axial, aligned roughly south-west, with large portal stones and a flat 'axial stone' opposite.

Standing Stones

Of widespread occurence, these vary in height up to a maximum of around 5 metres. The periods and purpose of their creation is somewhat obscure; this would not necessarily be the same in all cases. Tomb-markers, Sign-posts, Commemoration-stones or objects for ritual practice, the standing stones may have fulfilled all of these functions. Some are obviously phallic in appearance, others appear in what some describe as 'male' and 'female' pairs.

Still others have inscriptions written on them in

Ogham Writing

which is an ancient alphabet consisting of dots and strokes cut along the edge or edges of the stone. The majority of ogham stones are in Counties Cork, Kerry and Waterford, frequently also found lying flat or used as lintols in souterrains or other later structures.

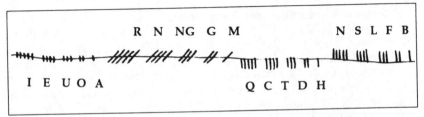

The Ogham Alphabet

In addition to the circles , single and pairs of stones, there are

Alignments

Found in two groups, mid-Ulster and Cork-Kerry. Ulster alignments tend to be made up of a large number (up to 25) of low stones, those in Cork-Kerry are of larger stones, but smaller in number. Aligments tend to be in areas commanding a wide view and tend to be run in a northwest-southwest direction.

Holed Stones

A certain number, not great, of stones have holes perforated through them. Usually round, fist sized, the holes' purpose is not clear though there is a definite connection with folklore about fertility, childbirth and love-making. Hands were clasped through holes to seal love bargains. Pieces of cloth were also passed through and, in certain cases, a healer would lay hands on the afflicted through the hole.

Bullauns

These are hemispherical depressions cut in rock or loose bounders, from fist-sized to up to 50 cm in diameter and half as deep. Their function is almost certainly ritual and magical. In modern times they are used in association with turning/cursing stones. These are loose, usually ovoid coconut-sized stones placed in the bullaun. These are 'turned' in certain manners for purposes of prayer, healing or cursing, dependent on local tradition.

Petroglyphs

Patterns and decorations carved or inscribed on rock or loose boulders which are likely to be associated with Bronze Age people. Motifs include concentric rings, spirals and circles. Interpretation of the 'meaning' of these occupy many but convincing explanations are slow to emerge. It is generally felt that they were of magical/ritual significance.

LOCATION OF MONUMENTS

The Map shows the county divisions of Ireland, with major towns and centres marked ●
On the following pages there is a county-by-county listing of selected monuments.

LOCATION OF MONUMENTS

For each county there is an entry detailing major examples of different monuments to be found. Obviously there are vastly more than listed, this gazatteer aims merely to show a satisfying variety. Firstly, in **bold type,** is listed the type of monument. There follows (in plain type) the name of the nearest town or village, then *(in italics)* the distance the monument is from that location. Distances are given in miles. Finally, again in **bold type,** the name of the particular townland where the monument is situate. These townlands are the basic topographical unit in Ireland, not generally shown on maps but known widely in their own locality.

Remember: The majority of monuments listed are on private lands. Well-disposed visitors are usually welcome. It was once believed that unknown gods or spirits would afflict those interfering with the structures. This may still be so but also nowadays it is a serious legal offence to interfere with them in any manner of means.

County Antrim:

Holed Stone: Doagh, *1 mile west of;* **Doagh** holed stone was used traditionally by lovers to pledge themselves by holding hands through the hole.

Stone Fort: Cushendun, *11/4 miles north of;* **Altagore** fort had diam. of 15 metres.

Portal Tomb: Carnlough, *5 miles sw of;* **Ticloy** dolmen is known as the 'Stone House'.

County Armagh:

Hill Fort, Armagh, *2 miles west of,* **Eamhain Macha** *(aka* **'Navan Fort'),** important mythological centre and seat of rulers of Ulster; Eamhain is an 18 acre fort enclosed by a bank.

Stone Figures: Armagh, in City (Protestant) Cathedral; the **'Tandragee Figure'** is likely the God 'Nuadu', also here are some 6 other carvings of heads from iron-age era.

Court Tomb: Newry, 4 *miles south of,* **Clontygora** 'King's Ring' is a 3 chambered court tomb. Remains of another nearby.

Portal Tomb: Camlough, 41/2 *miles SW of;* **Ballykeel** dolmen.

Cairn: Meigh, 1/2 *miles west of;* **Clonlum** cairn *(3 miles from Ballykeel above).*

County Carlow:

Standing Stone: Tullow, 11/4 *mile SSW of;* **Ardristan** stone is 'grooved', several examples of this type occur in the region of N. Carlow, S. Wicklow and S. Kildare.

Holed Stone: Tullow, 2 *miles south of;* **Ahade** holed stone is knows as 'Cloch a Phoill' which means 'holed stone'! Nearby here at **Cullaghmore** is remains of a Portal Tomb.

Portal Tomb: Tullow, 41/2 *miles NE of;* **Haroldstown** Dolmen.

County Cavan:

Stone Forts: Blacklion, 3 *miles SSW of;* **Moneygashel** is location of 3 cashels and a sweathouse

Ritual Structure: Ballyconnell, 3 *miles SW of;* **Killycluggin** megalithic structure, plus associated structures in **Kilnavert** and **Lissanover,** are likely to be associated with the pagan God 'Crom'.

Bullauns: Blacklion, 11/4 *miles W of;* **Killinagh** is a Christian monastic site created over an earlier settlement.

County Clare:

Ritual Site: Tulla, *31/4 miles SW of;* **Magh Adair** has several monuments, including mound and standing stones. An ancient pagan religious centre, in historical times it was the inauguration site for local rulers.

Wedge Tomb: Kilfenora, *4 miles E by S of;* in Burren; **Ballyganner South** is the largest in the area, others in the vicinity.

Stone Forts: Kilfenora, *21/2 miles NE of;* **Caharcutteen** fort is adjacent to several others, also tombs and dwelling sites.

Ogham Stone: Killaloe; *The (Protestant) Cathedral:* site of a unique 'literary' Ogham stone with bilingual inscription on both Ogham and Norse Runes.

County Cork:

Ogham Stone: Coachford, *41/2 miles NW of;* **Coolineagh** stone is associated with cures; a nearby boulder and well have mystical significance.

Stone Circle: Glandore, *11/2 miles east of;* **Drombeg** Circle and 'Cooking Place'; other circles nearby at Bohonagh and Reanascreena South.

Holed Stone: Kilcrohane, *33/4 miles WSW of;* **Caherurlagh** stone is associated with cures.

Stone Fort: Castletownshend, *3/4 mile west of;* **Knockdrum** Fort encloses an area 22 metres in diameter.

Wedge Tomb: Coachford, *61/2 miles NNW of;* **Knocknagoun** tomb.

County Derry:

Stone Circle: Dungiven, *31/2 miles SSW of:* at **Aughlish**, a group of circles and alignments.

Standing Stones: Claudy, *3/4 miles WNN of;* at **Cregg**, a 1.8 metre high stone known as the 'White Stone'. Another at Portrush, *11/2 miles SSW of here,* the **Carnalridge** 'White Wife' stone is of phallic significance.

Portal Tomb: Maghera, *1 mile NW of;* **Tirnoney** tomb has adjoining standing stone.

Cairns: Claudy, *11/4 miles NE* of; **Ballygroll** has remains of cairns, also wedge and court tombs.

County Donegal:

Stone Circle: Raphoe, *2 miles south of;* at **Tops, Beltany** Cairn and Circle.

Standing Stone: Muff, *1 mile NNE of;* **Ardmore** Standing Stone is a 2 metre high block decorated with Early Bronze Age Art.

Stone Fort: Greenan, *on the mountain so named;* **Grianán of Aileach** is a major structure associated with the ruling O'Neill family and earlier, as a 'Sun Fort', connected to pre-history/mythology.

County Down:

Portal Tomb: Dromara, *4 miles south of;* **Legananny** dolmen is one of Ireland's most striking examples.

Decorated Boulder: Churchtown *(near Strangford);* **Ballyculter Road** boulder is decorated with probable Bronze Age art.

Stone Circle: Downpatrick, *21/2 miles south of;* **Ballynoe** is a large circle, over 50 stones, and associated barrow.

County Dublin:

Portal Tomb: Killiney, *1/2 mile SSE of;* **Ballybrack** dolmen, with 'cup-mark'.

Standing Stones: Saggart, *3/4 mile SE of;* **Boherboy** standing stones are paired male and female, localled nicknamed 'Adam and Eve'.

Wedge Tomb: Dublin, *8 miles SSE of City;* **Ballyedmonduff** wedge tomb.

Portal Tomb (2), Howth, *in grounds of castle on Rhododerdron Walk,* **Howth** Dolmen.

County Fermanagh:

Stone Circle: Kesh, *41/2 miles NNE of;* **Drumskinny** circle and alignment.

Court Tombs: Boho, *2 miles SW of;* **Aghanaglack** is a double court tomb.

Carved Figures: Kesh, *6 miles E by S of, (3 miles SSW of Pettigo, Co. Donegal);* **Boa Island** figures include one likely to be of the pagan goddess Badb.

County Galway:

Stone Fort: Aran Island, *4 miles west of Kilronan;* **Dún Aonghasa,** major promontary fort. Other forts on the island are the **Dún Eochla, Dún Eoghanacht** and **Dún Dubhchathair.**

Cult Stone: Loughrea, *33/4 miles NNE of;* at Bullaun, the **Turoe** phallic stone is Ireland's finest example of La Tène carving.

Alignment: Dawros Bridge, *1 mile NW of;* **Derryinver** alignment consists of 6 stones orientated East-West.

Portal Tomb: Gort, *3 miles NNW of;* **Crannagh** dolmen. Nearby a **Wedge Tomb** at **Ballynastaig.**

County Kerry

Stone Fort: Caherdaniel, *beside village;* **Caherdaniel Fort** encloses an area 25 metres in diameter. Another fort, one of Ireland's finest, is *(7miles ESE of Waterville)* at **Staigue.**

Ogham Stone: Dingle, *21/4 miles ESE of;* **Emlagh East** Stone reads BRUS CCOS MAQQI CALIACI...M...

Stone Circle: Lauragh Bridge, *11/2 miles NE of;* **Drombohilly Upper** circle.

Bullauns: Kenmare, *51/2 miles SE of;* **Feaghna** multiple bullaun with associated phallic symbol and turning/cursing stones.

County Kildare:

Standing Stone: Naas, *21/4 miles SE of;* **Punchestown** stone is one of Ireland's tallest at 6 metres high. Another nearby at **Craddochstown West** and another in ritual site at **Furness** *(3 miles from Punchestown).*

Holed Stones: Castledermot, *in churchyard,* two holed stones, plus a pillar with cupmark.

County Kilkenny:

Portal Tomb: Harristown, *1 mile west of;* **Kilmogue** dolmen is known as **'Leac an Scáil'**.

Ogham Stone: Gowran; *In the (Protestant) church;* a stone reading MAQI ERACIAS MAQI DIMAQA MUCO (I).

Fort: Rathealy Ring-Fort has a raised circular area in centre, surrounded by a 20 foot deep ditch. Another Ogham Stone at **Tullaherin,** near round tower.

County Laois:

Bullauns: Borris-in-Ossory, *2 miles NNW of;* **Clonfertmulloe** multiple bullaun is known as 'St Mo-Lúa's ' stone from a saint associated with nearby monastic site. 'St Mo-Lúa's Bell', also from here, is in the British (for some reason) Museum.

County Leitrim:

Court Tombs: Manorhamilton, *3 miles SE of;* the two **Tullyskeherny** tombs are on straight lines (leys?) connecting Carrowmore (Co Sligo) and 'St Patrick's Chair' (Co. Tyrone).

Portal Tomb: Fenagh, *1/2 mile north of;* **Fenagh Beg** dolmen is located close to a cairn and a passage tomb. (Bone pendants found here are in the Dublin National Museum).

County Limerick:

Passage Tomb: Galbally, *11/2 miles WNW of;* **Duntryleague** tomb.

Stone Circles, Standing Stones, Tombs, etc:
Bruff, *21/2 miles north of;* **Lough Gur** is a major site with a concentration of monuments.
Brochures/Maps/Guides available at location.

County Longford:

Standing Stone: Ballymahon, *31/2 miles NNW of;* **Cartonbrack** is one of several in the area, others at Glenmore.

Portal Tomb:
Granard, *6 miles NNW of;* **Agnacliff** is a dolmen with 2 capstones.
Another nearby is at **Cleenrah.**

Stone Circle: Granard, *2 miles NE of;* **Cloghchunel** enclosure is likely the remains of a circle, another *(11/2 miles SSE of here)* at **Cartonore.**

County Louth:

Souterrain: Kilkerley, *1/2 mile south of;* **Donaghmore** Souterrain is one of Ireland's best-preserved examples with some 75 metres of passageway.

Portal-Tomb: Dundalk, *31/2 miles NE of;* **Proleek** is a noted tripod dolmen.

Holed Stone: Ardee, *2 miles SSW of;* **Hurlstone**.

Decorated Stones: Dundalk, *5 miles WSW of;* **Ballinloughan** petroglyphs, unusual design.

County Mayo:

Ogham Stone: Killala, *3 miles NNW of;* **Breastagh** stone.

Wedge Tomb: Ballina, *41/2 miles ESE of;* **Carrowcrom** tomb.

Cairn: Cong, *3 miles east of;* **Ballymacgibbon** cairn is 30 metres diam, 7 metres high.

Field Systems: Ballycastle, *nearby;* **Céide Fields** is a major archaeological site showing ancient habitats beneath the bog surface.

County Meath:

Ogham Stone: Kells, *31/2 miles WNW of;* **Castlekieran** stone *(in graveyard).*

Cemetery: Slane, *3 miles SE of;* **The Boyne Cemetery** includes the three well-known Passage Tombs of Newgrange, Knowth, and Dowth.

Stone Circle: Kells, *10 miles W by N of;* **Loughcrew** passage tomb cemetery includes numerous monuments, originally probably up to 100 tumuli. Graves, Cairns and decorated stones abound.
The circle is in **Ballinvally** townland.

County Monaghan:

Portal Tomb: Newbliss, *5 miles NE of;* **Garran** dolmen is in an area of several remains. **Carn court tomb,** *1 mile away,* **Tiredegan** double court tomb, *2 miles away,* and **Cloghernagh** court tomb, *4 miles away.*

County Offaly:

Bullauns: Tullamore, *3 miles SSE of;* **Meelaghans** bullauns are known as the 'nine-hole-stone'.

Sacred Site: Kinnitty, *near, at* **Clareen; Seir Kieran** is remains of a Christian monastery built on site of pagan ritual centre where a 'perpetual fire' burned.

County Roscommon:

Cult Stone: Roscommon Town, *4 miles SW of;* **Castlestrange** stone is an egg shaped boulder decorated all over in La Tène style.

Portal Tomb: Boyle, *2 miles west of;* **Drumanone** dolmen.

Ritual Sites: Tulsk, *3 miles NW of;* **Rathcroghan** crossroads is centre of a wide area of monuments, mainly earthworks, associated with the Goddess/Queen Medb.

Sacred Caves: Tulsk, *near;* **Glenballythomas Cave** is Oweynagat, otherwise the 'Cave of the Cat', the entrance to the Otherworld.

County Sligo:

Cemetery: Ballinafad, *21/2 miles NNE of;* **Carrowkeel** Passage Tomb Cemetery is a major site with numerous monuments. Another similar is at **Carrowmore** *(2 miles SW of Sligo Town).*

Holed Stone: Carrowmore, *at NW of cemetery:* **Tobernaveen** stone.

Portal Tomb: Ballyfarnan, *41/2 miles WNW of;* **Carrickglass** dolmen.

Cure Stones: Dromahair, *13/4 miles WSW of;* **Killerry** stones were used, in association with 'straining thread' to cure ailments.

County Tipperary:

Inauguration Site: Cashel; The **'Rock'**, now heavily Christianised, was formerly the power centre of local pre-Christian rulers.

Wedge Tomb: Inch, *11/2 miles NE of;* **Knock-curraghbola** Commons tomb, another *(6 miles south of here)* at **Baurnadomeeny.** There are several Standing Stones in the vicinity of this latter tomb.

Court Tomb: Rear Cross, *adjacent to village;* **Shanballyedmond** tomb, one of the most southern examples of this type.

Bullauns: Tipperary Town, *31/2 miles south of;* **Gotavoher** bullaun stone, colloq.'The Blessed Stone'.

County Tyrone:

Portal Tomb: Castlederg, *31/2 miles SW of;* **Leitrim** dolmen.

Souterrain: *At* **Aghnahoo,** *beside above.*

Stone Fort: *At* **Leitrim,** *close by dolmen above.*

Ritual Centre: Clogher, *4 miles ESE of;* **Altadaven** is site of various mysterious structures known colloq. as 'St. Patrick's Chair and Well'.

County Waterford:

Passage Tomb: Matthewston; a passage grave. Near here *(21/2 miles NNE)* is **Gaulstown** dolmen.

Ogham Stone: Carrick-on-Suir, *2 miles SE of;* **Ballyquin** stone reads CATABAR MOCO BIRIQ-ORB, translated by some as 'Battle-head tribesmen of Chariot-man'.

Portal Tomb: Waterford City, *4 miles SSW of;* **Knockeen** dolmen.

Passage Tomb (2); Dunmore East, *2 miles NNW of, at Fairybush Crossroads,* **Harristown** tomb.

Souterrain: Kilmacthomas, *31/2 miles SW of;* **Drumlohan** souterrain was constructed with 10 Ogham stones, some now erected in display.

County Westmeath:

Standing Stones: Ballymore, *3/4 mile S by W of;* Snimnagorta stone is known as 'Clogstuckagh', meaning 'prominent stone'. Another with the same colloq.name is *(3 miles SSE of here)* at **Moyvoughley.**

County Wexford:

Portal Tomb: Enniscorthy, *6 miles SSW of;* **Ballybrittas** dolmen.

Heritage Park: Wexford, *21/2 miles WNW of;* **Ferrycarrig** Heritage Park has a number of reconstructed examples of Irish buildings from the Stone Age up to the 13th Century.

County Wicklow:

Stone Circle: Hollywood, *11/2 miles south of;***Athgreany** circle of 14 stones, colloq. 'The Piper's Stones'.

Ogham Stone: Wicklow Town, *51/2 miles S by W of;* **Castletimon** stone reads NETA CARI NETA CAGI.

Hill Fort: Tullow (Co. Carlow) *3 miles east of;* **Rathgall** fort dates from Late Bronze Age (1000 BC).

Passage Tomb: Kilbride, *31/2 miles south of;* **Seefin** tomb.

PART TWO

IRISH MYTHOLOGY

INCANTATION TO IRELAND

I am the Wind that blows over the sea;
I am the Wave of the Ocean;
I am the Murmur of the billows;
I am the Ox of the Seven Combats;
I am the Vulture on the rock;
I am a ray of the Sun;
I am the fairest of Plants;
I am a Wild Boar in valour; I am a Salmon in the Water;
I am a Lake in the plain;
I am the Craft of the artificer;
I am a Word of Science;
I am the Spear-point that gives battle.
I am the God that creates in the head of man the fire of thought.
Who is it that creates in the head of man the fire of thought ?
Who is it that enlightens the assembly upon the mountain, if not I?
Who tells the ages of the moon, if not I?
Who shows the place where the sun goes to rest, if not I?

Amergin

The poem is from Amergin's incantation to Ireland, with origins perhaps five hundred years before Christ. In the poem Amergin, a Milesian warrior, as well as poet, and Ireland's 'First Druid', takes on the spirit of Ireland and speaks for its soul. Originating in north-west Spain's Galicia, the Milesians (see also page 40) are the ancestors of the Gaels who conquered the country and became the dominant tribe. Their essentially pantheistic earth-based religion, (what modern man might call 'New Age'), formed the basis of spirituality until the coming of Christianity; they retained political power at Tara until the arrival of the Anglo-Normans.

Mythology, what's it all about ?

MYTHOLOGY IS HOLISTIC HISTORY. It merges the story of events with that of spiritual experience and understanding. A blend of the magic, and the mundane, of darkness and of light, mythology portrays humanity as a whole. It spans generations, linking ancestors to descendants, identifying friends, warning of enemies, connecting peoples to their territories.

Fiercely tribalistic, nationalistic, pantheistic, animistic, chauvinistic, mythology contains a whole lot of these 'istics', these characteristics considered dangerous and undesirable by various establishments. The ideas in mythology are subversive, it is felt, they undermine the proper order of things. They cannot be classified. Neither bureaucracy nor religion can be built upon them. Such free-floating ideas are dangerous. In reality, of course, neither 'properness' nor 'propriety' have anything to do with mythology. It just is. Apart from judgements, it is morally neutral. More reason for disliking it. Those who order modern man's affairs and thoughts counter mythology by a combination of ignoring it and, when it inevitably emerges, damning it as sheer nonsense, and likely the work of the devil, to boot !

But the answer to that question, Irish Mythology, what *is* it all about ? Big question, small page. But certainly we do know it's all about a far wider world than merely Ireland or the Irish. As with religions, at the heart of all mythologies there is a universal, a simplicity, a flame of truth. Throughout the world this flame has ignited very different fires. At the heart of these fires the flame remains the same.

Irish mythology is Celtic mythology. The Celts are a people who appear in recorded history in the sixth century BC, though their migrations took place at a far earlier date, over a period from around 2000BC. From their base in central Europe, they spread westwards to the Atlantic coast, into Spain, and northwards to Britain and Ireland. Later they moved south to Italy, east along the Danube, reaching Galatia in Asia Minor. A multi-ethnic collection of peoples, from our vantage point we can look back and see them linked by language and art, and by a common opposition to Imperial Rome. We see them like this because we understand language and art, and we know how political systems clash, blend, and change. Our grasp of spiritual forces is less precise. We have no idea *why* the Celts created their particular mythology. A garrulous, aggressive, argumentative but imaginative people (sound familiar ?) the Celts were, in fact, exceeding strange.

Their mythology mirrors this strangeness. Nothing here is quite what it seems. One picture is the frame of another. An idea moves aside, to reveal a question. The answer to the question may be a joke, or a nonsense, or it could be true. But if it is true, you may have been deluded. And if it is a joke, you may be laughing at yourself. You will never know precisely, but you will find yourself increasingly fascinated and interested in learning more. To learn, of course, you have to be given the opportunity. And up to recent years modern western man (a category which includes the Celts, despite contrary propaganda !), modern western man has not been given this opportunity to learn about his mythology. Different machine-made Gods have occupied his attentions. Now, these Gods rusting, decrepit, running out of fuel, man is digging around in what remains of his spirit, searching.

This search frequently leads to an awakening of interest in the old Gods and Goddesses, and to attempts to understand just what it was the ancients believed, what made them tick. We find that though early man knew nothing of our sciences and systems, he was very far from being ignorant. Knowledge obscures, just as it reveals. Modern man has an immense store of knowledge. . . and little or no understanding of what it means. Ancient man didn't know very much, but throughout the world he came up with a strangely coherent set of ideas. The old Gods and Goddesses went by different names in differing societies and cultures, but on analysis they turn out to be much the same.

Here, though distinctly Irish, our Irish pantheon will be instantly recognisable to most Europeans. Not surprisingly, because most Europeans have Celtic blood.

This part of ANCIENT IRELAND is a basic guide for those that know next-to-nothing about Irish Mythology, but who want to know more. Do not be deluded, this is a difficult subject. Learning about it is difficult, and not least because heavyweight scholars and academics are lurking round every corner waiting to bore you to death.

The following pages establish a framework upon which understanding may be built, and a base for further study and research. The intention is to stimulate the curious, to help the searcher, to add wonder to the wonderer. It will. That's what this part of the book is about. But the answer to our original question, Irish Mythology, what is it about ? Perhaps the answer to that is best left to the reader.

A stone idol from Togher, near Finnea, Co Meath.
National Museum, Dublin.

EARLY IRISH SOCIETY

The fact that there are great gaps in our knowledge of the past should not lead us to the conclusion that there was chaos and anarchy. Early Ireland was a highly structured society. Ruled by a warrior aristocracy, the grades of this society ranged downwards through the military nobility, the craftsmen, and the peasants.

The military were the *flaithi,* patrons of the craftsmen, who were the *oes dána,* a category which included poets, lawyers, historians and doctors as well as metalworkers and so forth. The proletariat were the *grád féne,;* lowest on the rung were slaves, a male being known as a *mug,* a female as a *cumhal.* Many *cumhals* were concubines and influential people in society.

The *filé,* 'poet', was a member of the craftsman class and his position has dictated the type of mythology that has been passed down to us. Generations of these professional storytellers were attached to the courts and households of both prominent individuals and factions and their stories naturally concerned the doings of the leading classes. What the masses were up to, we have little idea. We do know that they were tied to their overlords by a complex system of mutual obligation, but of their way of life, their ideas, little has emerged. The actual link between classes were particularly noteworthy. Not serfs, the lower orders could separate from their overlord, he from them likewise, provided certain conditions were met.

Groups of families made up *tuaths,* and groups of these made up the provincial kingdoms. Anciently there was five of these but until around the eleventh century AD there was no 'High King'. Each province was autonomous. Gratifyingly there was no 'civil service' or bureaucrats other than single individuals known as *rechtaire,* in charge of revenues. A special judge, *Bretim Ríg,* supervised the king to ensure he stayed within the law. The legal system was sophisticated but incomprehensible to modern man in that there was no state law as such. Order was maintained by a system in which transgressors answered to the transgressed. Individuals were assigned 'value'; relatives would be compensated accordingly. Owed money, a man would sit outside his debtor's house, starving himself. The debtor was put under an obligation to himself starve until the matter was resolved. If he ignored the hunger-striker he lost honour. If the striker died, the debtor was more or less an outcast so complete was his loss of honour. And this was the nub. In their society this 'honour' occupied much the same position as money does in ours. Without honour, a man was living in the ancient equivalent of cardboard city.

TYPES OF TALES

Primarily oral, the tales were passed down by *Filid*, professional story-tellers that were usually attached to local rulers and kings. Translated as 'poets', the filid were in fact quasi-druids, retaining many of the aspects of that class of society. 'Satire' from a *filé* was regarded in the way modern man would regard a 'spell', dangerous to one's health and well-being. The stories themselves were part of ritual and were magical instruments in their own right. One particular druidic characteristic inherited by the filid was the prohibition on committing their knowledge to writing. All had to be retained in the memory.

At around the 12th century AD the tales were formally divided into *Prímscéla* (Main Tales) and *Fo-scéla* (Subsidiary Tales). A *Filé* would know 250 main tales, 100 of the subsidiary. The tales were classified as

Togla	- Destructions	*Echtrai*	- Adventure Journies
Tána	- Cattle raids	*Aitheda*	- Elopements
Tochmarca	- Wooings	*Airgne*	- Slaughters
Catha	- Battles	*Tormadmann*	- Eruptions
Uatha	- Caves	*Slúagaid*	- Expeditions
Immrama	- Voyages	*Tochomlada*	- Immigrations
Aitte	- Deaths	*Físi*	- Visions
Fessa	- Feasts	*Serca*	- Love-tales
Forbasa	- Sieges		

Modern scholars have classified the tales into four groupings, described latterly as 'cycles'. These are

Mythological Tales	- The Mythological Cycle
Heroic Tales	- The Ulster Cycle
King Tales	- Cycle of the Kings
Finn Tales	- Fenian Cycle

However, as understanding grows of the relationship between 'mythology' and 'history', many now feel that such classifications are more hindrance than help towards enlightenment. Tales, themes and characters weave in and out of the arbitary 'cycles' imposed upon them. 'Real' historical personages appear here as humans, there as Gods, all is flux and flow, and understanding must come from a deeper source than that offered by academic classifications.

THE MANUSCRIPTS

Christianity brought to Ireland the habit of scribes, monks and scholars recording information in manuscript form. The stories of mythology, hitherto passed down orally (*see* Types of Tales, *page 33*) were now written down in monasteries and places of Christian learning. Although drawn from the same class as the poets and bards of the old order, these educated Christians were obviously determined to impose a Christian veneer upon the pagan tales. Odd references to Christian themes abound, and a particular effort was made to ensure that the chronology of the Tales fitted into the Biblical scheme of things. That noted, the surviving early manuscripts are in fact the only source available to us, as, with the collapse of the Gaelic Order in the middle ages, the educated oral tradition faded away, surviving only in patches of folklore and superstition. The manuscripts that survive largely bear evidence of themselves having been copied from older books now lost, as indeed is the bulk of early Irish literature, mainly destroyed in the 17th and 18th centuries by deliberate policy of the English Penal Laws in efforts to eradicate Irish culture. Huge numbers of books had already been destroyed between the 8th and 11th centuries during the Viking raids. All our main surviving manuscripts date from after that period. These major manuscripts are the following:

LEABHAR NA hUIDRE
known as
The Book of The Dun Cow.
This is an 11th Century manuscript apparently compiled at Clonmacnoise. It is now in the Royal Irish Academy.

LEABHAR LAIGNEACH
translated as
The Book of Leinster.
This is a 12th Century manuscript compiled at a monastery in Terryglass, Co. Tipperary. Housed in the Royal Irish Academy.
It also contains the
DINNSEANCHAS,
meaning
'The Lore of Placenames',

(cont'd above right)

which is a topography of Ireland
and a guide to geographical mythology.
This also contains a version of

LEABHAR GABHALA,
translated as
'The Book of Invasions'.
(This appears in several mss.,
of which there is a 17th century
compilation by Micheál O'Cléirigh).

THE BOOK OF BALLYMOTE
is a 14th Century manuscript
also in the Royal Irish Academy.
This contains
The Book of Rights.

THE YELLOW BOOK OF LECAN
is another 14th Century manuscript
housed in Trinity College, Dublin.

THE GREAT BOOK OF LECAN
is a 15th Century manuscript
housed in the Royal Irish Academy.

'RAWLINSON MS B502'
is the catalogue name of an important
manuscript housed in
Britain's Bodleian Library.

In addition to these there are many other manuscripts to which scholars refer. Surprisingly, some 70 years after Ireland's re-emergence as an independent nation, there are many hundreds more which remain unedited or untranslated. The scholars Kuno Meyer and Eleanor Hull calculated around the year 1900 that there were up to 300 tales and sagas buried forgotten in unresearched manuscripts - the majority of these remain in similar condition today. That noted, a massive amount of work has been carried out on the manuscripts, not least by non-Irish researchers in the latter part of the last century and the early part of our own. This work includes direct translations into modern Irish, English and other languages, plus commentaries and analysis.

CONTENT OF TALES

❚❚ The doorkeeper saw an unknown troop approaching him. A fair and shapely warrior, with a king's trappings was in the forefront of that band. They bade the doorkeeper to announce in Tara that they had come. "Who is here?" said the doorkeeper. "Here is Lug of the fierce combats, son of Cían son of Dían Cécht, and of Ethniu daughter of Balar; he is the fosterson of Talann, daughter of Magmór King of Spain, and of Echaid the Rough son of Duí."
The doorkeeper asked the Samildánach: "What art dost thou practice? For no one without an art enters Tara". "Question me," he said: "I am a wright." The doorkeeper answered: "We need no wright. We have a wright already, Luchta son of Lúchaid." He said: "Question me, doorkeeper: I am a smith." The doorkeeper answered him: "We have a smith already, Colum Cúailleinech of the three new processes." He said: "Question me: I am a champion." The doorkeeper answered: "We need thee not. We have a champion already, Ogma son of Ethliu." He said again: "Question me: I am a harper." "We need thee not. We have a harper already, Abcán son of Bicelmos whom the Men of the Three Gods entertained in sídmounds." He said: "Question me: I am a warrior." The doorkeeper answered: "We need thee not. We have a warrior already, Bresal Echarlam son of Echu Báethlám." Then he said: "Question me, doorkeeper: I am a poet and historian." "We need thee not: we have a poet and historian already, En son of Ethoman." He said: "Question me: I am a sorcerer." "We need thee not. We have sorcerers already; our wizards and men of power are many." He said: "Question me: I am a leech." "We need thee not. As leech we already have Dían Cécht." "Question me," said he: "I am a cupbearer." "We need thee not. We already have cupbearers, Delt and Drúcht and Daithe, Taí and Talam and Trog, Clé and Glan and Glése." He said: "Question me: I am a good metal-worker." "We need thee not: we already have a metal-worker, Credne the Metal-worker." He spoke again saying: "Ask the king whether he has one single man who possesses all these arts, and if he has I shall not enter Tara."
The doorkeeper went into the palace and declared all to the king. "A warrior has come before the garth," said he, "called Samildánach; and that one man possesses all the arts practiced by thy household so that he is the man of each and every art." "Let him into the garth," said Núada; "for his like has never before come to this fortress."
Then the doorkeeper let Lug pass him, and he went into the ❚❚ fortress and sat in the sage's seat, for he was a sage in every art.

This passage is from the oldest version of the tale *Cath Maige Tuired,* *(see* Battle of Moytura, *page 59).* It is believed to be oral-based material from the ninth century, written down in the 11th or 12th centuries in a mixture of Old Irish and Middle Irish languages, and preserved now in a 16th century manuscript, British Museum Catalogue Harley 5280, f63 sq. The title of this version of the tale is *Cath Maige Turedh ocus Genemain Bres Meic Elathain ocus a Ríghe,* meaning 'The Battle of Moytirra, and the Birth of Bres Son of Elathan and His Reign.' The tale has been edited and translated by Whitley Stokes.

We learn something of the complexities of the manuscripts and the difficulties of their language from these details noted. However, analysis of content shows a rewarding richness and depth.

The passage quoted notes the coming of Lug from Eamhain to help the Tuatha dé Danaan in their hour of need. Lug is the *Samildánach,* meaning the 'master of all crafts'. He is of course perhaps the most important of Gods, The Sun God *(see page 44).* Dian Cécht is the God of Medicine. and Balar (or Balor) is lord of darkness. Thus we see the Sun-God, born out of darkness, arriving at the headquarters of the Tuatha dé Danaan to help them fight those same forces of darkness. Those who told these tales, as those who listened, would know these references automatically, much as modern western man would understand Biblical nuances. Each reference in the passage has hidden meanings. The 'Three Gods' were the Trí Dee Danaan, the three Gods of artistic skills who prepared the weapons for the dé Danaan to use against the enemy Fomorians. The 'síd-mounds', actually the burial places of previous cultures, were regarded by each succeeding civilization as the dwelling places of the Gods. (*Síd* can be translated as 'fairy', giving us such words as 'banshee', fairy-woman). Dian Cecht, whilst being the God of Medicine *(see above)* was also a human druid skilled in the science, 'a leech'. (Modern man may find it difficult to understand how an individual may be both 'druid' and 'god' but the sheer time scale of events should be remembered. Christian saints are revered, even prayed to. . . and not long ago they were human). The practice of medicine was regulated under the old Irish system of law, The Brehon Law, by a tract called the 'Judgements of Dian Cecht', much as modern western medicine refers back to the 'Hippocratic Oath'. Nuada was the ruler of the dé Danaan. After the First Battle of Moytura, in which he had lost a hand, Dian Cecht gave him a silver replacement that he might remain 'whole' and thus retain the kingship. He thus became known as 'Nuada of The Silver Hand'; (Nuada was killed by Balor in the Second Battle of Moytura).

(For details of Núada, *king of the dé Danaan, see page 48).*

LAND AND LANDSCAPE:

Ireland itself takes its Irish-language name from Éire, a Goddess of the dé Danann. She was the wife of Mac Gréine, his name meaning 'Son of the sun'. Mac Gréine's father was Ogma, a son of Dagda, the 'Father of the Gods'. Ogma is associated with the Celtic God known as Ogmios, of eloquence and literature.

Éire's 'sisters' were Banba and Fódhla, between them forming a triune Goddess, each representing differing aspects of the whole. Banba and Fódhla's names are sometimes used in poetic reference to Ireland; as example, ships of the modern Irish navy have been frequently given these names.

Éire's human origins are as Eriu, Queen of the dé Danaan, daughter of Fiachna; Eriu was slain by Suirge the Milesian at the Battle of Teltown in 1698 BC.

Names of places and topographical features very frequently take their names from characters or events mentioned in the stories of mythology. Much of this harks back to a time when mountains and rivers were regarded as living creatures, the physical embodiments of Gods. The mountains known as The Paps (near Ballyvourney) in Co. Kerry, for example, take their name from the Irish *Dá Chich Anann*, the two breasts of Anu. This Anu was the Goddess from whom the Tuatha dé Danaan take their name. Similarily the River Boyne takes its name from Boand, a particularly ancient Goddess-entity associated with moon-worship. She, a water-goddess, mated with Dagda, the great God, producing the son Aengus, God of Love. (Newgrange, through which thousands of tourists troop, is actually the grave of this Aengus). Towns and villages, though more often their names record Christian saints, frequently recall very ancient events. Thurles in Tipperary, as example, takes its Irish name (Durlas Eile) from Eile, a young woman burned alive on a fire as a sacrifice. Names of localities, particularly in remote spots, recall ancient entities.

Lackcrom, a forest near Donegal Town, is actually *Leac Crom*. A *leac* is a flagstone associated with worship, Crom is *Crom Dubh* or Black Crom, a powerful ancient God to whom human sacrifices were offered.

PEOPLES, TRIBES & RACES

Mythology concerns itself much with the interreaction between different groups of people, whether living in differents parts of Ireland, or between the indigenous and the new arrivals. Expressed generally in terms of military struggle, there are underlying themes of cultural and religious wars. To establish precisely who the different factions were is not easy. Earlier peoples tended to be considered as supernatural by later cultures - while the Gods of these earlier ones might be considered as human. This has confused modern observers. Essentially there is no reason to believe other than that all were, in their time, as real as modern Germans, Spanish or Canadians.

Ceasair's People:

These are said to be the first inhabitants, Ceasair being 'a daughter of Noah', she came to Ireland to escape the Flood. With her she brought fifty girls and three men and, dividing the girls among the men, they populated various parts of the island.

Fomorians:

A people with origins in Scandinavia, regarded as pirates, 'sea robbers' and settlers on coastal areas, their headquarters were on Tory Island off Donegal, their leaders being Bres and Balor. Their name is said to derive from 'beneath the sea' and they are generally regarded as a dark and violent race. They battled frequently with Partholónions, Nemedians and Tuatha dé Danaan, sometimes emerging as the victors, other times as the vanquished.

Partholonians:

Partholón was a descendant of Magog, the origins of these people being as Canaanites from the eastern Meditteranean. Credited with introducing agriculture, they cleared plains and fought the Fomorian inhabitants.

Nemedians:

Nemed arrived in Ireland from Scythia with four women, the only survivors of a fleet of over thirty ships from the Meditteranean. From this small base the new race grew to the extent of defeating the

Fomorians in battle. However, struck by both plagues and a resur gence of Fomorian power, the Nemedians were reduced to a remnant who, it is said, went to Greece. An unremarkable people, the Nemedians have left little trace of their existence. Britain, however, was a Nemedian, giving his name to a country to the east of Ireland. Macha (*see page 41*) was also one of the race. We do learn from them, nonetheless, the origins of Hallow'een 'Trick or Treat' customs, based on the fact that the Fomorians imposed a tax upon them to be paid at Samhain (s ee page 46).

Firbolg:

A people who came to Ireland after the Nemedians, some say they were survivors and descendants of the dispersed Nemedians, others that they were connected to the Belgae, a tribe of European Celts. Not involved greatly in the stories of mythology, chief interest focuses on their origins and on the meaning of their name. Firbolg can be translated as 'bag man', some saying this implies that they wore a particular type of trousers, others that they were a lowly caste of soil-carriers, using bags for that purpose. This latter theory is somewhat supported by the fact that the Firbolg were grouped with the Fir Gallion and the Fir Domnan, the latter being credited with the introduction of ploughing, their name meaning 'earth men'. Defeated by the Tuatha dé Danaan, the Firbolgs settled on Aran and Rathlin Islands. Also associated with them is Teltown in Co. Meath, named after Tailtiu. Not a Firbolg herself, she was married to one of their rulers, Eochaid mac Erc. Malahide in Dublin takes its Irish name *Inbher Domnain* from the Fir Domnan settlers there.

Milesians:

A people who take their name from Míl or Miles Hispaniae, 'a soldier of Spain'. These were the latest group of invaders to our own historical times and are considered to be the ancestors of the Gaels. The Annals of the Four Masters gives the date of the Milesian arrival as 1498BC, though modern scholars put it at nearer 500BC. It is recorded that Míl, who in fact was a Scythian mercenary soldier, served with the Pharoah Nectanebus. Pharoahs of this name ruled Egypt in the 30th Dynasty around 350BC. Míl married Scota. He personally did not reach Ireland but the conquest was carried out by his sons. Arriving in Kerry, they fought their way to Tara and overthrew the Tuatha dé Danaan, establishing themselves as rulers there until their own over-throw at the hands of the Anglo-Normans.

IMPORTANT CENTRES

Certain locations are frequently mentioned in the stories of mythology. The intermingling of mythology and history means that these centres were generally the power bases of particular rulers or groupings or, as former 'capitals' of distantly remembered ancestors, were religious or sacred sites used for seasonal gatherings.

Eamhain Macha:

Also known as NAVAN FORT, this location is central to the grouping of stories known as the Ulster Cycle. These are set in the first century AD and largely revolve around Cuchulainn, a warrior in the reign of the Ulster King, Conor mac Nessa.

Eamhain Macha was founded by, and takes its name from Macha Mong Ruadh (Macha of The Red Tresses), daughter of Aedh Ruadh. She was the seventy-sixth monarch of Ireland. Her father had alternated kingship with his two brothers and, on his death, Macha was elected ruler. Her uncles objected. In wars she defeated one, Dithorba, killing him, and persuaded the other, Cimbaeth, to marry her. It is said that Macha marked out the extent of the fort here with her brooch and forced the captives from the succession wars to build the structure.

Occupied from the Third Millenium BC, Eamhain Macha's history spans between four and five thousand years. Its important period was likely to have been Late Bronze/Early Iron Age, from around 700BC. Eamhain Macha was destroyed in 355AD by soldiers of the High King Muiredach, perhaps for religious reasons, the group involved being noted as having assassinated leaders and destroyed a Celtic religious centre in Co. Cavan.

Rathcroghan:

Known in mythology as *Cruachain Ai* and *Rath Cruachain*, this was a seat of the rulers of Connacht, particularly associated with Queen Medb. She, with husband Ailill, is reputed to have reigned here at the beginning of the Christian era. Not her principal residence, it is written that she came here at Samhain (Hallow'een) 'to confer with her magicians and her poets'. Perhaps the major centre of ancient Ireland, seventy prehistoric monuments have been identified by archaeologists in the area. These are noted as being of ritual origin and character; there are also a like number of residential structures dating from the

(Rathcroghan cont'd)

first millenium AD.
A cave in the area is regarded as
the entrance to the 'Otherworld'.
Location:
Over miles, on the road between
Tulsk and Frenchpark,
Co. Roscommon.

The Hill Of Allen:

Site of a great fortress built by
the druid Nuada, and the 'dwelling place of Fionn mac Cumhall".
This 676 foot high hill is the
ALLMHAIN of mythology.
Location:
8 miles NE of Kildare Town.

The Hill Of Uisneach:

The 'Centre of Ireland', a great
stone here marked the point
where the five historic provinces
met. A centre for the Feast of
Bel *(see page 20),* this is a site
associated with fire-cults.
Location:
Rathconrath, Co.Westmeath.

Tara

The *Temuir* of mythology, its
name comes from the Goddess
Tea, wife of Eremon, the first
Milesian High King. Regarded
generally as ancient Ireland's
'capital', structures here have
been dated back to 2000BC.
Location:
On the Dublin-Navan road,
Co. Meath.

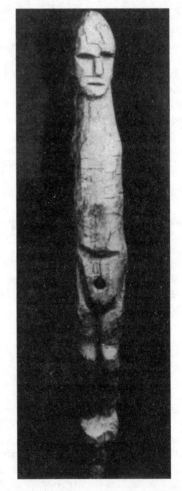

Wooden idol from Ralaghan, Shercock, Co Cavan.
National Museum, Dublin.

GODS & GODDESSES

A Celtic characteristic has been to make one's heroic ancestors into Gods and Goddesses, and equally to give one's Gods and Goddesses human characteristics. In the Irish context, where myth and history merge over a great span of time, where successions of invasions with different cultures and beliefs have been absorbed, it is not always easy to distinguish between 'real people' and 'gods and goddesses'. Further complications arise due to the ambiguous position of certain important 'peoples' in mythology. Whether the Tuatha dé Danaan were 'real' or were a race of Gods is a question much exercised. Were they the dispossessed people of an earlier cultural group, or were they the Gods of that group? These and similar questions arise more frequently than do satisfactory answers. But what is clear is that Gods and Goddesses generally were considered as ancestors rather than as creators of man. As such they were considered to be very like ourselves, subject to both human virtue and vice and prey to both our problems and our joys.

The Dagda

The Great God, the Father of the Gods, known also as the Lord of Occult Knowledge, the Dagda was leader of the Tuatha dé Danaan. He is portrayed as possessing a giant club, one end used to slay enemies, the other to heal friends. He also possessed a magical cauldron which could feed multitudes, a story which, though much earlier, is reminiscent of the Christian loaves and fishes. This cauldron, brought by the dé Danaan from their mysterious city of 'Murias', was one of their chief treasures. The Dagda took part in fertility rites with the Goddess Boand (*see below*) on the eve of Samhain (Hallow'een). He is buried in the Boyne Valley.

Brigid

A daughter of the Dagda, she is a 'triune Goddess', appearing in three forms or aspects as The Goddess of Healing, The Goddess of Smiths, and The Goddess of Fertility and Poetry. This is the 'Brigindo' goddess of the Gauls and the 'Brigantia' of the Britons. Her festival was held on the first of February, Imbolg. She is associated with the breasts of women and with human and animal lactation; she has as her symbol fire. Brigid's sacred fire, tended by female druids, burned at a location in Co. Kildare from ancient times until put out by the Normans. This fire, taken in conjunction with her swastika/sun wheel symbol, the

'Brigid's Cross', remind us of pre-Islamic Persian religions. Christian nuns, followers of the Christian Saint Brigid, tended the fire after Ireland's conversion to Christianity. The Saint herself, daughter of a Druid, was most likely a former priestess of the pagan Goddess.

Lugh:

A Sun-God, of arts and crafts, his grandfather was Balor of the Evil Eye. Lugh was father of Cuchulainn. He is the Welsh God *Lleu* and the *Lugos* of Gaul and he has given his name to many places throughout Europe, from Lyon in France, Leiden in Netherlands, to England's London (or Lugdunum). Lugh killed Balor, as prophesised, and was ruler of the dé Danaan for a short time. It is said that Lugh is the originator of the 'Leprechaun', the 'fairy craftsman' the word coming from Lugh-chromain, 'little stooping Lugh'.

Boand:

A water-Goddess, she has given her name to the River Boyne, her own name meaning 'White Cow Goddess'. She is associated with the moon, phases of the moon in mythology being represented by different colour cattle. Ptolemy described this Goddess as Buvinda. The wife of Elcman, she bore a son to the Dagda *(see page 50)*.

Balor:

The God of the Fomorians, associated with Tory Island off Donegal. Sometimes regarded as a 'God of Death, Balor had a malevolent eye which destroyed whoever looked at it. Thus he was called 'Balor of The Evil Eye'. Learning of a prophecy that he would be slain by his grandson, he looked his only daughter away in a tower. But this was unsuccessful and eventually he was slain by Lugh *(see above)*.

Manannán Mac Lir:

The God of The Seas, his name essentially meaning 'son of the sea'. Lir, also *'Llyr'* in Wales, gave his name to England's *Leicester* and also to Shakespeare's *King Lear*. The Irish *Manannán* has given his name to the Isle of Man. Associated with the dé Dánaan, Lir is indubitably a Sun-God, the association of sun-gods with sea-gods bringing us back to Chaldean times and remotest antiquity. The three-legged 'Isle of Man symbol' is allied to the Brigid's Cross, Swastika and other sun symbols.

FESTIVALS & FEASTS

In early Ireland the year was divided into two six-month periods by the feasts of Beltaine (also known as *Cétsamhain*) and Samhain; each of these two periods was itself equally divided by Lugnasadh and Imbolg. These four major festivals were essentially associated with the seasons and were commonly celebrated throughout the Celtic world; they also had their parallels in other world cultures.

Imbolg:

A festival held on the first day of February, associated with the Goddess Brigid, one of whose aspects was that of fertility. The word 'imbolg' derives from early-Irish language meaning 'sheeps' milk'; this being the date that ewes would come into milk for the coming season.

Beltaine:

Held on May Eve and the first day of May, this marked the start of the summer. The word is translated as meaning 'the fires of Bel'. The festival was observed by lighting bonfires, originally by druids using the rays of the sun. Domestic fires were extinguished and new fires kindled from these sacred fires. Cattle were driven between bonfires in purification rites. 'Bel' is generally held to be Bilé, the God of Life and Death, an important deity in the Celtic world. (London's 'Billingsgate' takes its name from Bilé). Bilé would have associations with Baal, the Eastern deity. The word also has associations with 'Crossroads'. The Roman festival of Compitalia was celebrated with sacrifices at crossroads at the same date - in Ireland the 'dancing at crossroads' phenomenon would have roots in observances of Bel.

Lugnasadh:

An August festival essentially, gradually it became associated with the last Sunday in July. This was the feast of the God Lugh, introduced by him to honour his foster-mother Tailtiu. A harvest festival, it was celebrated for fifteen days with games and merrymaking. Major events were held at Tailtiu's place, modern Telltown in Co. Meath. Though generally associated with merrymaking and courtship, boys making ceremonial garlands for girls and so forth, in certain areas the festival had more sinister overtones through its association with Crom, being known as Black Crom's Sunday. The major modern Irish

(Festivals & Feasts cont'd)

Christian pilgrimage takes place on Lugnasadh to Croagh Patrick; the month of August in modern Irish is *Lúnasa*.

Samhain:

A festival held from the evening of the last day of October until the following day. At this time it was believed that spirits from the Otherworld were let loose and wandered the earth, causing problems and difficulties for mankind. It is recorded that religious elements gathered taxes at this time, processing about the countryside in ritualistic activities and damaging the property of reluctant taxpayers. A complex festival of both fertility and sacrifice, the name simply derives from the early-Irish meaning 'end of summer'. Gods such as the Dagda became sexually active with both Goddesses and with human women: people reflected this activity in fertility rites. Certain women were immersed in water and then tested by fires. These may have been priestesses - the treatment of witches in later eras is likely an echo of these rites.

Celtic Calendars:

Although we recognise the feasts and festivals of the ancients, and to some extent still celebrate them, there was a different conception of the passage of time and of its significance. A completely different system of calendar was in operation. One such Celtic calendar (the Coligny Calendar, from the first century AD) demonstrates both the difference and the complexity of their systems. This was based on a table of sixty-two consecutive months, approximately amounting to five solar years. Months were of twenty-nine or thirty days and divided into halves. Thirty day months were 'auspicious', twenty-nine day months not so. However, certain days in an 'auspicious' month were not lucky, similarly certain days in the 'inauspicious' months were lucky. The second half of each month was characterised as 'returning night', the months thus divided into 'bright' and dark' halves. The full moon occurred on the seventh, eighth and ninth days of the month. Particular days in each month were related to those in a previous month by a system of transference and interchange to ensure that ritual would be carried out on days appropriate to the lunar/solar cycle.Every third year an extra month of thirty days was included to adapt the lunar year to the solar year. The days of this month had no actuality or names of their own, being merely a calculating device!

TÁNA & 'THE TÁIN'

Tána, meaning 'cattle-raids' are one of the main classifications of the tales known and told by the tenth-century filid *(see page 8)*. These were plundering expeditions in which one faction would carry off the cattle, (the wealth of those times) belonging to another. Woven into the simple story of the raids were many strands, telling of individual valour, of past events, of magic and the supernatural. The two best known Tána are *Taín Bó Fraoch*, 'The Cattle-Raid of Fraoch' and *Taín Bó Cuailgne*, the Cattle Raid of Cuailgne, known simply as

The Táin:

The Taín Bó Cuailgne is the great Heroic Epic of Irish literature. It is the central tale in the Ulster Cycle *(see page 33)* which deals with the doings of the warriors ruled over by Conor mac Nessa at Eamhain Macha (page 33). These, the Red Branch Knights, had as their hero Cuchulainn. Though such comparisons are vacuous, if the Taín is the 'Irish Iliad' (as often described,) then Cuchulainn is the 'Irish Achilles'. The Taín tells how the youthful hero held up an army of Connacht invaders whilst awaiting the arrival of the other Ulidians or 'Ulstermen'. These were held by a mystical illness known as the 'cess nóinden' in mythology, as a 'couvade' by anthropologists. (Being a type of purification rite endured by men after childbirth).
The Taín is an Heroic Tale of an Heroic Age. Heroic literature in all cultures is aristocratic; it admires qualities such as loyalty, prowess and honesty. The Heroes are idealised. Boasting is no fault. Description of war, and also of clothes, palaces and weapons are universal in Heroic Literature. And these are the elements that make up the Taín. The scholar Nora Chadwick pointed out that invariably where such literature exists there existed beforehand an historical Heroic Age. Evidence in the Taín, particularly the depiction of the Ulster warriors as fighting from chariots, a Celtic attribute of the 1st Century BC, dates this historical age at that period.
There are two versions of the Taín, an Old-Irish one based on 9th Century oral tradition and the Middle-Irish version written down in the 12th Century in the Book of Leinster. Modernisations appear in later manuscripts. Heavyweight scholars such as Thurneysen (*Irische Helden-unp Konigsage*) have analysed the old-Irish version; Cecile O'Rahilly has edited and translated both the Book of Leinster and Book of the Dun Cow versions. Numerous writers have presented 're-tellings' ranging from the magnificent to the farcial.

TUATHA DÉ DANAAN

Both the nature and the origins of these people are shrouded in mystery. They came, it is said, from the four fabulous cities of Falias, Gorias, Finias and Murias. arriving in a sea of cloud, or smoke, they brought with them both magical arts and sacred mysterious objects. Represented generally as people of goodness and light, the dé Danaan overcame both the 'dark' Fomorians and the Firbolg *(see page xx)* and established themselves as the rulers of Ireland.

Their name, Tuatha dé Danaan, has always been translated as meaning 'People of the Goodess Danu'. This Danu, also known as Anu or Ana, is regarded as the mother Goddess. She is mother of the Dagda *(see page xx)* and her 'husband' is Bilé, the God of Death. Certain early manuscripts, however, list Danu with Badb and Macha as 'The Sinister Women'. Interestingly the Irish language word 'Tuatha' can mean 'people' as in 'tribe' or can be an adjective 'sinister'. Elsewhere Dana is described as 'The Great Queen[. This description, Morrigan, became separated from her and 'The Morrigan' is now considered as a different Goddess. As Anu was originally, The Morrigan is 'The Goddess of War'.

The 'people' associated with Anu have sometimes been considered 'Danai', otherwise a class of Greeks, or 'Greco-Pelasgians' in the language of academia. Their origins in 'Northern Europe' have prompted others to consider their origins as being Finland; connections between that country and Assyria are documented. In Assyria-Babylon cultures a Danu was a major God.

Whatever about all that, Irish mythology tells us that their migration occured under Tabairn. They first settled at Magh Tabain, on the Clyde in Scotland. 'Five generations' later Nuada led them to Ireland, landing on the River Erne in Donegal. This was the famous *Nuada Argetlámh*, 'Nuada of the Silver Hand'. He lost the hand in a battle but, given a silver one by a druid, he remained 'whole' and could thus retain kingship. Over time, the dé Danaan leaders such as Nuada in effect became Gods. In other Celtic cultures Nuada himself appears as Llud and as Nudens. The original Gods the migration brought with them, and the actual leaders, merged together as a partheon of Gods. Then when the dé Danaan were overcome by the Milesians (the ancestors of the Gaels), it was felt they had moved underground and that they lived in raths and mounds. Folklore turned them into 'the Fairies'. But they have survived such ignominy to exert a strange and still unexplained psychic influence over Ireland.

LOVE & LOVE STORIES:

Whether 'love' or 'battle' is the major theme in Irish Mythology is difficult to decide. Many of the wars are caused by 'love'. All in all the tales present us with a picture of a society of completely different mores than our own. 'Honour', 'Pride' and 'Purity' are important values to the ancients, 'sexual morality' is not a concept dealt with. Men and women are equally earthy, swopping wives, lovers and husbands with ease. Complications were caused by the fact that there were ten different types of marriages recognised. Some of these were temporary, some permanent, and others for particular purposes and situations. Although in an essentially polygamous society, the women nonetheless appear to have had remarkable freedom in their activities. Female rulers would pick and choose among male warriors. Wives would bring a young woman into their husbands' beds as a gift. All this is recorded in a merry sort of attitude, problems only arising when 'honour' was affected. It is perhaps no coincidence that the two great love stories (below) are based on an affront to a proud ruler's 'honour'. Both stories also, of course, emanate from tribal systems and deal with challenges to the 'old male's' authority by younger blood.

Diarmuid & Gráinne

Diarmuid was a young warrior of the Fianna *(see page 51)*. In his youth himself and other warriors stayed in a hut in a forest with an old man, a sheep, a young girl and a cat. The tale has it that the sheep was 'the world', the cat was 'death', and the young girl was 'youth'. At night she made love to Diarmuid, marking him with a spot on his forehead. This 'love spot' had the effect of inspiring all women to love Diarmuid.

Fionn mac Cumhail, the leader of the Fianna, became betrothed to Grainne, daughter of the High King. Fionn was by now an old man, Grainne was not anxious to wed him and so seduced Diarmuid into elopement.

For sixteen years the couple wandered Ireland as fugitives from the vengence of Fionn until peace was made. The couple settled at Tara. Later, during a hunting expedition, Diarmuid was chased by an enchanted boar at Ben Bulben in Co. Sligo. The still vengeful old Fionn encouraged Diarmuid to do battle with the animal. . . and Diarmuid was killed. The body was taken by the love God *(see page 50)* Aonghus and brought to Newgrange. Aonghus promised to 'send a soul into him' and talk to him each day. This is the story, the bare

(Love & Love Stories cont'd)

bones of one of the great love stories of Irish literature. But not the greatest, which is

Deirdre Of The Sorrows

A story with similar theme to Diarmuid and Grainne, this tells of Deirdre, daughter of an Ulster chieftain. When she was born the druid Cathbad prophesised that she would bring death, war and destruction to Ulster. Conor mac Nessa was the king at the time and, pressed to kill the baby by his supporters, he instead said he would have the child brought up in seclusion and, when she was old enough, he would have her as a wife which would keep her out of mischief making. However, before she was married, Deirdre eloped with Naoise, a warrior of the Red Branch *(see page 51)*. They lived in Scotland until, assured of safety, they returned to Ireland. Here Conor attacked the Red Branch Knights, causing in effect a civil war in the Ulster kingdom. This ended in Naoise's death at the hands of Eoghan mac Durthacht. Conor took Deirdre as a wife but, after a year of bad temper from her, he told her he was sending her to be a wife to the warrior mac Durthacht. She was tied up and placed in a chariot but, en route, managed to throw herself out and be killed. She was buried beside Naoise. A tree grew from each of their graves, their branches inter-mingling overhead.

Aonghus

The son of the Dagda and Boann *(see page 43)* Aonghus Óg is the love-God of Irish mythology. He lived at Newgrange. Of beautiful appearance, from birds representing his horses always hovered about him. The 'Dream of Aonghus' is a celebrated love-story. In this he sees a beautiful maiden, falling in love with her. With help of the gods, he identified her as Caer, a daughter of the dé Danaan in Connacht. Aongus asked Queen Medb of that region to persuade the girl's father to give her to him. The father said that that would be for the daughter to decide and, in any event, she lived in the shape of a swan, along with a hundred and fifty other swans. It was up to Aonghus to identify her. This he did, and Aonghus and Caer returned to Newgrange where they lived together. This story of a love affair between human/god and woman/mystical bird has parallels in many cultures and variations on it lie at the heart of many world religions.

MILITARY ORDERS

Professional warriors were banded into elite military organisations, generally loyal to particular kingships, sometimes as mercenaries for hire. This was a lifetime career, boys being recruited at a young age, older men forming groups of veterans. In Munster there was the military Degad, in Connacht the Gamhanraide, but the most famous were the Red Branch and the Fianna. These warrior bands lived lives apart from the general community and were subject to different laws and obligations. They had certain extra rights, to live off the land (in effect to rob property) and to seize women for a particular variety of one of the recognised form of marriages.

Red Branch Knights:

Based at Eamhain Macha (*see page 41*), these were the guardians of Ulster and the elite soldiers of rulers, particularly of Conor mac Nessa in his reign. Cuchulainn (*see page 55*) was the great champion of the Red Branch. Their name derives from *Craobh Ruadh*, which actually was a huge red 'branch' or lump of timber supporting their ritual hall; this was a place of quasi-mystical rites, decorated with the skulls of their enemies. The activities of the Red Branch are recorded in the Ulster Cycle of tales. The main stories of this cycle include the **Táin** (Táin Bó Cuailgne) itself, developments and preliminaries of Táin themes, plus separate tales such as **Bricriu's Feast, The Intoxication of The Men of Ulster, Mac Da Thó's Boar** and **The Fate of The Children of Usna.**

The Fianna:

These were the warriors protecting the High Kingship, based at Tara. A military caste drawn from particular families, the Clan Bascna and the Clan Morna. Their best-known leader is Fionn mac Cumhaill. The activities of Fionn form the basis of many tales in mythology, for many modern Irish they *are* mythology. This grouping of tales is known as the Fenian Cycle, and it includes **The Pursuit of Diarmuid and Grainne** (*see page 49*)and **The Battle of Ventry.** The Fenian Cycle was synthesised in the 12th.Century into a work known as *Acallm na Senórach*, 'Colloquy of The Ancients'. The Fianna, said to be founded in 300BC, eventually grew so powerful as to become a threat to the High Kingship. This lead to the Battle of Garristown where they were defeated and dispersed.
(*See* Gabhra, *page 59*).

THE DRUIDS

This was a learned class, both men and women, involved with secular and religious proceedings. Distributed throughout the Celtic world, Julius Caesar came across them in Gaul and wrote an oft-quoted (perhaps too oft-quoted) piece on them. But briefly:

❚❚ The Druids are all under one chief, who possesses the supreme authority in that body. Upon his death if anyone remarkably ex cels the rest he succeeds; but if there are several candidates of equal merit, the affair is determined by plurality of suffrages, sometimes they even have recourse to arms before the election can be brought to an issue. The Druids never go to war, are exempted from taxes and military services, and enjoy all manner of immunities. These mighty encouragements induce multitudes of their own accord to follow that profession; and many are sent by their parents and relations. They are taught to repeat a great many verses by heart, and often spend twenty years upon this institution; for it is unlawful to commit their statutes to writing, though in other matters, whether public or private, they make use of Greek characters. They seem to follow this method for two reasons: (1) to hide their mysteries from the knowledge of the vulgar; and (2) to exercise the memory of their scholars, which would be apt to lie neglected had they letters to trust to, as we find is often the case. . . They teach likewise many things relating to the stars and their motions, the magnitude of the world and our earth; the nature of things, and the power and prerogatives of the immortal gods. . . In threatening distempers and the eminent dangers of war, they make no scruple to sacrifice man, or engage themselves by vow to such sacrifices, in which they make use of the ministry of the Druids; for it is a prevalent opinion among them that nothing but the life of a man can atone for the life of a man, insomuch that they have established even public sacrifices of this kind. Some prepare huge colossuses of osier-twigs into which they put men alive, and setting fire to them, those within expire amidst the flames. They prefer for victims such as have been convicted of theft, robbery, or other crimes,believing them the most acceptable to the gods; but when ❚❚ real criminals are wanting, the innocent are often made to suffer.

Caesar and other Romans, also the Greeks, wrote much in this vein on the Druids, some of it far from flattering... though it must be remembered that to the Classical civilizations the Druids were rival authority figures among the barbarians. Ireland, of course, was largely unknown to the Classical writers. In the context here many modern scholars have felt that the Druids were mere wandering magicians. They do appear to have arrived rather late in the scene. Some feel that they were driven out of Gaul and Britain by the advance of the Roman Empire, making they way to the safety of Ireland. Obviously theirs was not the only scientific or religious system. Earlier religions will have survived; some of these existing alongside, others giving elements of their beliefs to the ideas of the druids. There are grounds for believing that many of the recorded wars and struggles had a religious base. Information on our Druids comes generally from Christian scribes who also had reasons for denigrating their spiritual predecessors. It is thus difficult to form a picture of the reality. Certain things stood out in the Irish context which can be noted. Druids here were primarily involved with magic and supernatural affairs, rather than teachers; they appear also to be closely involved with rulers, often being of the same class or married into the ruling class. Women druids are prominent and druidism appears to some extent to be hereditary. The later *filid* (*see page 33*) appear to have inherited certain functions. Certainly their method of memorising rather than committing to writing the corpus of knowledge comes directly from the habit of the druids. Early Christians in Ireland were quasi-druidical, to the extent that there were female 'bishops' and that early monks adopted the Druidic form of tonsure of the hair.

Overall then we see that the *activities and functions* of the Druids are fairly well documented; from classical and native sources we can form a coherent picture. Similarly the *origins* of Druids are known, it being generally accepted that they share a common Indo-European inheritance with the brahmins of India. Striking similarities do exist between both groups, and the resemblance between the Irish and Indian law books has been noted by scholars. The Irish *derbfine* (the family grouping made up of four generations) is the same as the Indian *sapinda*. The Irish marriage laws are parallel to the Indian, as is a system of inheritance through an appointed daughter's offspring, the *putriká* in India being the same as the Irish *ban-chomarba*. The system of hunger-strike mentioned (*page 32*) is common to Indian law also and linguistically certain words associated with religion and kingship are the same in both Indo-Iranian and Celtic languages.

Tanderagee Idol, Armagh Cathedral.

RELIGION, BELIEF & SACRIFICE

While we know the activities, origins and functions of the Druids, the actual religion they taught is unknown. The Gods and Goddesses *(see page 43)* are documented, not so the precise beliefs or forms of worship. It is difficult for modern man to systemise the apparantly isolated, sometimes contradictory elements known about the religion of the ancients. Mother Earth was worshipped as a source of fertility, being understood as a triple divinity. This three-headed divinity is depicted in numerous effigies and is common to many cultures. Ireland had a triple natured war goddess and, representing this, in certain situations three sacrificial women were loosed among warriors before battle. Naked, bedecked with bird feathers, and tied together at the neck, the three victims were chased about, warriors hacking at them with swords so that they became splattered with blood; all this to create a sense of excitement and blood-lust for the forthcoming fight. This barbaric treatment of women should not be construed by modern feminism to imply that women were oppressed. Far from it, society was almost matriarchal in form and many major leaders were women. Britain's Celtic Cartimandua and Boudicca and Ireland's Medb are particularly noted but women generally and the female spirit or Goddess were paramount. The male Gods all had what Indians call a *Sakti,* a female 'source of power'. The dominance of the female element led to the situation of female priestesses, ruled by female rulers, sacrificing female victims. Male sacrifices met equally grisly ends. Hung upside down, the priestesses (again!) cut captured warriors' throats and collected the blood for arcane religious purposes.

Both male and female victims were hanged, stabbed and drowned, simultaneously, for complex ritual purposes. A remnant of this practice survived in England up to the eighteenth century AD when people were 'hanged, drawn and quartered'. *(Part Three of the present book deals in more detail with these topics)* On a more tranquil note, the Druids were noted for their recognition of the sacredness of particular places, particularly groves of trees. Individual trees were worshipped and ritual applied, as were wells, rivers, stones and features such as vallies and mountains. In addition to the Boyne *(see page 43)* the River Shannon was also a Goddess *(Sinainn).* The particular peoples of mythology *(see page 39)* each had particular sacred animals, the Firbolg had the pig, the dé Dánaan cherished the horse. The ancestors of the modern Irish, the Milesians, held the thorn bush sacred. . . modern Irish still cherish this 'fairy tree'.

CHAMPIONS & HEROS

The heroic deeds of individual warriors are central to very many tales in mythology. Many of these are grossly exaggerated to the realms of fantasy, giving powers of incredible skill and stamina to the champions. The role of champion was defined and official, he took precedence over other warriors, sat at a certain place and got 'best cut', the 'champion's portion' of meat at a feast. Jealously guarded, the champions themselves fought over this role, much honour and pride being at stake. In the story of Mac Da Thó's Pig, a dispute between the Connacht champion Cet mac Mágach and that of the champion of Ulster gives rise to a typical exchange.

" 'Go away from that pig', said Conall. 'What should bring you to it?' said Cet. 'Truly', said Conall, 'that is to challenge me to a contest! I will contest with you for once, Cet,' said Conall. 'I swear the oath of my tribe, since first I took a spear in my hand I have not passed a single day without killing a Connachtman, nor a night without setting fire, and I have never slept without a Connachtman's head under my knee'. 'It is true', said Cet, 'you are a better warrior than I. If it were Ánluan who were in the house, he would contest with you. It is bad for us that he is not in the house'. 'But he is', said Conall, taking Ánluan's head from his belt. And he hurled it at Cet's chest so that blood flowed from his mouth. Cet went away from the pig, and Conall sat down by it."

The result of all this was when Conall proceeded to take the best part for himself, and gives out to the Connachtmen the fore-legs of the pig, they rise from their seats and there is a general battle after which 'corpses are heaped upon the floor and blood is flowing through the doorways'.

Bloodthirsty, truly, but complex and stylish, with more than a hint of humour, the tales of champions and their heroic deeds offer an insight into the Celtic world. Innumerable individuals are mentioned in these tales, Cúchulainn and Fionn mac Cumhaill perhaps best remembered now, their names and identities somewhat blended in the modern consciousness as a symbol of the 'Irish Hero of Long Ago'.

Cúchulainn

Up to about the eleventh century, Cúchulainn was the national hero of Ireland, a central character in the stories of the Ulster Cycle (*see page 33*). His mother was Dechtire, daughter of the druid Cathbad. Taken away by mystical birds, she returned pregnant with a child, Setanta. Setanta grew up to be a warrior and, one day, at a feast, he killed a hound belonging to Culann, a smith. Smiths were a dangerous, close-knit guild or faction and, to save himself, Setanta said he would take on the guard role of the dead hound. Thus he became 'The Hound of Culann', or in Irish, Cúchulainn. Many tales are told of him. In reality, a picture emerges of a ferocious and almost pathological character, the heads of slain enemies dangling from his chariot, cutting a swathe through human and god alike. He was involved with many women, particularly Emer, daughter of Fogall The Wily. Of his many battles, The Táin (*see page 47*) is most noted. Of his single combats, his slaying of his best friend Ferdia stands out. In the end of his career, after rejecting the love of the Goddess of Battle, he was killed, fighting to the last, supported upright by being tied to a pillarstone, slashing out furiously at his enemies. Many concepts in these stories go back to primative Indo-European beliefs. A light (*'luan láith'*) plays around Cúchulainn's head in battle - we may know this as the 'halo' of Christian saints. Rivers rise up to protect against the invaders, and Gods lead a hand where necessary.

Fionn Mac Cumhaill

Belonging to a later era, Fionn is the central character in the Fenian Cycle of Tales (*see page 33*). Whilst Cúchulainn, above, was champion of Ulster, Fionn's loyalty was to the High Kingship at Tara. Son of Cumal of the Clan Bascna, a military grouping, Fionn became leader of the Fianna and, after the eleventh century, his tales and doings became the popular element in mythology; reflecting of course the growth of the High Kingship and a central authority. He was educated by Finegas, a druid on the Boyne. Fionn's name means 'Fair One'. Like Cúchulainn, his deeds include excellence in all human activities, and some distinctly non-human. His dogs were the offspring of his sister, another story! And his son Oisín was the child of a faun. One of his earlier exploits was to rescue a bag containing the treasures of the Fianna. This bag was made out of the skin of the woman Aoife. The flavour of the majority of Fionn tales is equally fantastic; they generally appear to be rehashed from half-remembered older themes of earlier times. It is not entirely comforting to learn that Fionn, far from being dead, is asleep in a cave, waiting to return to help Ireland in case of emergency.

POPULAR STORIES

Though Irish Mythology is not 'popular' in the sense that few know anything about it at all, a few certain stories are commonly known, told and re-told, their themes and motifs being used in many situations and by artists of various disciplines *(see page 60)*. These stories, listed below, occur frequently in children's books, as do such notions as the 'fairy ring' (a rath), and the 'fairy tree', (a hawthorn bush). The 'banshee' is also mentioned. Little else arises generally. The fact that mythology is full of sex and violence might be thought a reason for its neglect in popular culture. . . until we realise that the very popularity of TV is based on such content. Essentially it transpires that Irish Mythology is neglected because it is 'pagan'. Neither 'Christian' nor 'Materialist', it presents a world-view which has been culturally unacceptable. It is the weakening of the Christian-Materialist system that has unleashed the present day interest in the topic.

The Children Of Lir

Aobh and Aoife were two of the daughters of Ailill of Aran. Aobh married Lir, the God of The Ocean *(see page 44)* and bore him a daughter, Fionula, and three sons, Aodh, Fiachra, and Conn. After Aobh's death Lir married Aoife who, jealous of the children, turned them into swans. Aoife herself, in revenge for this, was turned into a vulture by Bodb Dearg (Bodb the Red), a major God. She was condemned to spend eternity in the skies. The swan-children had to spend 900 years as swans, three hundred in County Westmeath, three hundred on the seas between Ireland and Scotland, and three hundred off Erris in the West of Ireland. There, turned back into humans, though ancient and decrepit now, they died. They are buried on the Mayo Island of Inish-glora.

Oisín

A son of Fionn *(see page 56)*, Oisín was a poet and warrior of the Fianna. A beautiful maiden appeared one day, Niamh of the Golden Hair. She was a daughter of Lir and invited him to accompany her back to the Land of Promise, a name for the Otherworld, world of the spirits. Ni-amh had an enchanted horse and she and Oisín travelled away on this. In the Otherworld they had several children, Oscar, Fionn and a daughter called 'The Flower of Women'. Lonely for Ireland, Oisín returned on Niamh's magic horse. She warned him not to dismount.

Oisín returned to find that 300 years had passed since his leaving, the Fianna were no more and the Christian era had commenced. He travelled about Ireland for a while and then one day fell from the horse by accident. Immediately he turned from a golden youth into a withered old man. In this form he wanders about, meeting St. Patrick and generally lamenting. When he died he was buried in the pagan druidical manner, wrapped in the hide of a black bull, facing east, near Manorhamilton in Co. Leitrim.

The Salmon Of Knowledge:

Over a mystical well grew nine hazel trees of wisdom. The nuts fell into the water and were eaten by the salmon Fintan. The salmon made his way to the River Boyne where he was caught by the Druid Finegas. Finegas gave it to his pupils to cook. One of these was the youth Demna, son of Cumal, a leader of the Fianna. Demna brushed his thumb against the cooking salmon and sucked at it to relieve the burn. He thus acquired wisdom or more precisely, a type of 'second sight' where he could 'see' what was happening in distant places. This boy Demna was later named Fionn (The Fair One) son of Cumal, Fionn mac Cumhaill (*see page 56*). Throughout his life, when he wished to have 'second sight', otherwise *fios*, a type of mystical wisdom, all Fionn had to do was to suck his thumb.

Such are the bare bones of three well-known popular stories from Irish mythology. The first two are, of course, archetypical examples of folklore to be found throughout the world - the story of Rip Van Winkle will be familiar to most. In the Children of Lir this is overlain with a 'bird motif' not particularly Irish itself, but common in stories; people frequently change or are changed into birds. The imaginative have related this to the idea of spaceman/birds appearing as 'Gods' to the 'primitives'. Whatever. The Salmon of Knowledge is more complex and 'Celtic' in character. The notion of wisdom residing in sacred wells is a recurring theme; even in modern folklore many 'Holy Wells' are reputed to hold a particular 'sacred fish', usually a salmon or trout. The notion of sucking one's thumb to acquire insight may be of antique origin. Frequently wise men are depicted in carvings as sucking their thumbs. This could be related to the chewing on raw sacrificial flesh which was a druidical method of bringing on a trance; whilst forming one's body into a circle (viz Rodin's sculpture 'The Thinker') no doubt has eastern religious origins in relationship to the flow of bodily forces. Our tales are not so simple as they seem!

BATTLES

War and battle were an integral part of all Celtic societies. Ferocious fighters and 'head-hunters', the Celts were noted for the frenzied savagery with which they attacked an enemy. Despite this frenzy, whipped up by recourse to particular Goddesses of Battle and encouraged by sacrifices and divinations by priestesses, the battles were carried out with a certain ritual akin to chivalry. It is this behaviour that is chiefly recorded in mythology, with much emphasis on the skills and feats of particular champions and heros.

The Battle Of Moytura:

Magh Tuiread, variously translated as the The Plain of Towers or The Plain of Weeping, is site of two of the great battles of Irish mythology. The confusion of the translation of the name has been equalled by that allied to the location of the plain itself and, indeed, who took part in the battles. Modern Moytura (Moytirra) is in North Sligo near Lough Arrow and this is perhaps nowadays generally felt to be the site of the battles. The other location mooted has been around Cong in County Mayo. There, it is said, the first battle was fought between the Firbolgs and the dé Danaan (*see page 40*). The second battle, definitely at Sligo, took place between the dé Danaan and the Fomorians (*see also page 39).* The dé Danaan won the first, driving the Firbolg out of Ireland to isolated islands. The second was a more complex affair. The rulers of the dé Danaan and the Fomorians were intermarried and essentially the same caste. It does seem, however, that the dé Danaan had some aspects of a subject people and the battle represented a rising up against unpopular overlords. The story of the battle is heavily overlaid with mystical imagery; it is not difficult to see that this was a struggle between distinct religions and value systems. The dé Danaan won, under their leader Lug (*see page 44*). Nuada, another of their kings, was slain here, as was Balor ('of the Evil Eye') leader of the Fomorians.

The Battle Of Gabhra:

This took place at Garristown in Co. Dublin between the forces of the High King and the Fianna. The latter, fomerly a type of elite force (*see page 51)*to protect the kingship, had grown out of hand and now threatened it with its own power. Cairbre was King at the time, while the Fianna were led by Oscar, Fionn mac Cumhaill's grandson. Both these died in the battle,which is said to have taken place in 284 AD.

ANCIENT IRELAND

MODERN IRELAND

ATLANTIC ISLAND

http://www.atlanticisland.ie

IRELAND
ON THE INTERNET

PART THREE

MAGIC, RITUAL & RELIGION
IN ANCIENT IRELAND

THE CREATION

When the upper region was not yet called Heaven,
And the lower region was not yet called Earth,
And the abyss of Hades had not yet opened its arm,
Then the chaos of waters gave birth to all of them.
And the waters were gathered into one place.
No Men yet dwelt together,
No animals yet wandered about,
None of the gods had yet been born,
Their names were not spoken,
Their attributes were not known.
Then the eldest of the gods,
Lakhnu and Lakhamu, were born,
And grew up.
Assur and Kissur were born next
And lived through long periods.
Anu was born . . .

from the 'Creation Tablet' of the Chaldeans
c. 2000BC

The text above will show the span of time with which we are dealing. Around 2000BC was by no means the begining of the Red Sea Chaldean civilization, nor was it the start of things in Ireland. Magic, ritual and religion stretch over aeons. In this section of the book the entries relate to different periods over a span of thousands of years. Comparatively modern folklore and superstition. . . alongside the primal concepts of most ancient man. It is for the reader to draw the connections.

Magic, Ritual and Religion, which is which ?

MAGIC HAS ITS ROOTS in the psychic powers generated by groups of people. Ritual is the system which links the world of magic to the everyday. Religion is the means by which society controls magic. The balance between magic, ritual and religion determines the type of society that is created.

The balance and relationship between the three is not static. Magic becomes ritual. Ritual becomes religion. And religion becomes part of the social system. This is a path of growth, change, and decay; it is predictable and sure as a seed becomes a tree, a tree turns into a lump of wood, and the wood becomes a chair. . . or a coffin.

A lot is known of ancient Ireland. Irish mythology is rich and complex. We have stories and tales of Gods and Goddesses, of Wars and Heroes, Laws and Genealogies. But. . . despite, perhaps because of this richness, it is not easy to unravel the essential beliefs of the ancients. It is not easy to separate the magic from the ritual, or to see where these end and the glum grind of religion takes over.

It is said that Christian monks censored the ancient texts, making them difficult for us to interpret. Maybe so, though many of the early Christians were not far removed from being Druids themselves. And much of Irish Christianity was merely a skilful adaptation of earlier systems. Now, in our day, we see this clearer. As the tide of Christianity recedes we begin to see its bare bones, rather as the bare bones of some great dead beast might be revealed in a dried-up lake.

Perhaps we should look at those bare bones, spare a moment to look at Irish Christianity. We see huge crowds climbing sacred mountains on particular days. Pilgrimages to wildernesses and visions of virgins are popular. As are treks to distant lands to follow reports of miracle and wonder. Nothing to do with Christianity, really, these bare bones. They belong to an earlier era, they are part of the magic and ritual of the ancients.

We refuse to recognise this. Modern Western Man is under the impression that he lives at the peak of development, that all that has gone before was merely a preparation for this, now, here we are, all the junk rejected, contained neatly in our culture all the wealth of human experience.

But there we are. Back to those bare bones, bits and pieces of ancient magic, ritual and religion too, scattered here and there with no apparent connection. Experts on dinosaurs can wire together a reasonable shape from scattered skeletons. Not so easy with belief and behaviour or human systems. Certainly there are specialists, historians, archaeologists, anthropologists, linguists, but their very specializations acts as blinkers to their understanding.

At this point in the Western World the elements of magic and ritual in our spiritual inheritance are at a low ebb. Only at the extreme branches of Christian/Moslem fundamentalism or New Age occult/satanism are magic and ritual taken seriously. Spirituality, for the masses, is something called religion; a system, and a fairly unmagical and bureaucratic system to boot. This religion, the end result of the process where magic and ritual evolve, this could act as a support or a hindrance to society. Priestly classes can be essential links between man and the mystical beyond. . . or perhaps as now, in our western world, mere functionaries in the niche markets of birth, marriage, and death. The modern Christian religion has a hollow feel. On weekdays most churches contain more collection boxes than people. Those collection boxes rattle with the music of Christianity's successor religion, Materialism. Here is a belief that money can solve all problems. Unfortunately for everyone, Materialism itself is threshing around in its death agonies.

(Continued overleaf)

The world is watching, aghast, amazed, paralysed as the great dying system destroys individuals, nations, whole continents, endangering the very earth itself. Obviously our civilization will die long before the planet does but that is not much consolation to the individual. But perhaps life itself has never brought much consolation to the individual, and this is the reason for the restlessness. Backwards and forwards, progress or reverse we cannot say except that there is some process at work.

Looking at the past we see that same process, the process by which magic, ritual and religion blend and change, one becoming the other, we realise that, just as in the modern world, this has always been so. There have been periods of ignorance, experimentation, knowledge, and arrogance. Once we understand this, things become clearer. Not much clearer, it must be said, but at least we have a framework within which to be confused.

Understanding of magic and ritual is a thing of the spirit. Acceptance of religion is a social decision. We cannot accept magic in the same sense as we accept the diktats of fashion. Spiritual growth is achieved in little stops and starts, by hints, nuances, the unexpected. And even by the sudden unwelcome understanding.

This next section of the book is made up of pages of such stops and starts, hints and nuances. The format is deliberate. There is no thread, nor narrative, no argument. Some topics are more substantial than others; but just because some are dealt with shortly does not mean they are less important. (It may merely mean that the writer knows less about them !) A number of topics are dealt with at greater length because they are central to the Magic, Ritual and Religion of the ancients. It is no accident that these very topics are parallelled in modern concerns. The interaction of mankind as a whole on the environment, the relationship of groups of people with their place (for whom we can read *tribe, nation* or *ethnic group*) and the relationship between male and female, the balance of these forces both within individuals and in society.. this is what the modern world is all about.

In the listings starting on the facing page,
entries are ordered alphabetically;
where headings use Irish-language words, these are italicised.

A

AIRBE DRUAD

A mystical protective barrier ('druid's hedge') created round an army by a druid. It sometimes seems that a similar barrier protects the ancient wisdoms and understandings from ourselves: but read on . . .

ANU

King Tigleth-pilesser was a special adherent of Anu. An Assyrian ruler of 1130BC, this king would have recognised a triad or three-person God made up of Anu, Bel, and Hea. Anu and Bel were brothers, Hea was a 'Holy Spirit', with no family connection, but of equal power. Anu was ruler of the earth. Bel controlled the heavens. Hea's dominion was the sea and, more than that, the ethereal cosmos that surrounded creation.

These Gods are very old. The roots of Hea are in Chaldean antiquity, several thousand years before Tigleth. The Chaldean culture, where writing was invented, was based on the shores of the Red Sea. The civilization spread from there to Babylon, Assyria, Jerusalem. The Chaldean mythology has it that their skills were brought to them by OE, a fish-human personage who emerged from the waters. We can read of all this on surviving clay tablets.

Anu, (whose 'sign' was a single upright wedge, and whose 'mystical number' was sixty) was a male. But he had a wife, Anata, a shadowy personage whose own attributes are forgotten or unrecorded. This lack of definition is essentially because she *was* him, his female self, his original. All Gods were at one stage Goddesses, their sex having changed to suit the changing dominant principle. For some time now our own Gods have been male but a shift is under way as we become more 'earth-centred'. Unfortunately our new female Goddesses, by themselves, will do little to improve the quality of life. This depends on the balance between male and female.

In Ireland, anciently, Anu remained female. Same God, different sex. All the major Celtic Gods are, in fact, female. Even those that are male have a type of female guiding force looking over their shoulder.

Anu is our Mother Goddess and Earth Goddess. Her name is sometimes Ana, or Dana, or Danu. The Tuatha dé Danaan are one of the 'races' or 'peoples' of ancient Ireland. God-like, their leaders are, in effect, the Gods of Ireland. Generally regarded nowadays as benign and the 'powers of light', their name *Tuatha dé Danann* is translated as meaning 'People of the Goddess Anu'.

While one automatically assumes one's Gods to be benign, evidence for the nature of the *dé Danaan* is not conclusive.

While the Irish-language word *tuath* does mean 'people' or 'tribe', it can also mean 'sinister, perverse, malign, evil'. The word *'tuathal'* implies spell-making and witchcraft, and the conjuring up of sinister forces. In one of the most ancient of the Irish manuscripts there is a description of Anu, along with her two 'sisters' Badb and Macha, as *'na ban tuathige'*, meaning 'the sinister women'. In one of his battles the Hero Cuchulainn was supported by entities associated with Anu. *"Ra gairester imme baccanaig, ocus bananagaig, ocus geniti glinni, ocus Demna aeoir"*. "The satyrs, and sprites, and maniacs of the valleys, and demons of the air shouted about him. . ."

None of this sounds particularly 'benign' to this writer. Further, we know that in Britain Anu was worshipped as Andate. The ceremonies involved the suspension of sacrificial women in groves of trees and the severance of their breasts which were pinned up about the place in grisly fecundity rituals. Breasts as symbols of nourishment are important to Anu. In Ireland's County Kerry we have placenames such as *The Paps of Anu* and *The Paps of Morrigan*, this latter being a poor translation from *Da Cich na Morigna*, actually meaning the Two Breasts of the Great Queen. Eerily echoing this, we remember that in Egyptian religion their source of life, the Nile, was said to originate at a place called Questi. This place was shaped like two breasts. This is perhaps too slim evidence to believe that the Nile rose, or was thought to rise, in County Kerry but it has been postulated that elements of Egyptian culture arrived from elsewhere in a completed system. The Nile, as source of life, could very well have led through folk memory to some Atlantean past, some misty memory of the mountains of Kerry. We must keep our open minds, even at the risk of appearing absurd. Another Egyptian - Irish connection concerns bulls. In Egypt Anu is said to have created a bull at the request of Ishtar, this bull being involved in titanic struggles. Stories of struggles between great bulls are central to much of Irish Mythology. A four-thousand year old Chaldean spell to protect against the Evil Eye is translated as 'Spirits Anunna-ge, Great Gods (Protect us)'. The 'Great Goddess' of Ireland is Morigna, 'sister' of Anu. Morigna is a Goddess of War. Aeron (a river name in Wales) is the Goddess of Slaughter. Anata is the Egypto-Semitic Goddess of War. She is depicted as a naked woman standing on a lion. She wears a crown of bird feathers. Morigna, the Irish

Goddess of War, appears as a bird. In the East she is also Anahita, associated with Mithraism, a religion deeply involved with caves. In Ireland she emerges from the Cave of Cruachan *(see page 71)*. She emerges, half woman, half terrible animal . . . a lion?

ASTROLOGY

Early Irish astrologers were known as *néladoir*, meaning 'cloud diviner'. These examined the skies for auguries, signs, and portents. One of their particular functions was to tell the appropriate time to commence building a house. Later, in our own historic middle ages, the Zodiac *(see page 105)* as understood internationally was examined. An ancient Irish one of these is preserved in Basle, Switzerland. This contains breakfast-television type astrological predictions.

B

BAN-TUATH-CAECHA

'Women blind in the left eye'; these were regarded as messengers of Fate. Cuchulainn met three of them on his way to battle. A trio of gruesome crones, they were cooking pieces of a charmed dog on spits of rowan wood. They are connected to the *Ban Tuathige*, the sinister woman personae of the three goddesses, Badb, Macha, and Ana. Shakespeare utilised them as the three prophesying witches encountered at the start of his Scottish play.

BOARD GAMES

Games, something like modern cribbage, were played by the Irish and other Celtic peoples. The original use of these 'games' was for divination and ritual rather than recreation. *Fidchell*, frequently mentioned, is said to have been invented by the God Lugh of the Tuatha dé Danaan. Other Irish games were *Branfad* and *Brandubh*, both of these names inferring an association with ravens. Brandubh in effect means 'Black Raven'. In Welsh tradition (in the Mabinogion) a board game between Arthur and Owein has as background a struggle between men and ravens. Ravens or Crows are symbols of the Irish

(Board Games, cont'd)

Goddesses of Battle, the Morigna. The movement or presence of particular birds are constantly noted as augurs by Druids; certain birds were sacrificed and examined, cocks were buried alive. (The wish-bone custom of modern chicken-eaters is a survival of all this). Man recreates his memories of struggle and search in the form of recreation. Just as modern football represents battle, Celtic *Fidchell* was formerly a sort of ouija board for communicating with spirits. One of Ireland's main 'treasures', it is recorded, was 'The Board of Crimthann'. This was brought from 'the depths of the sea'. Crimthann himself was slain by 'magic women', (war-Goddesses) at Samhain. Even more thought provoking, one of Britain's treasures, ('Royal Jewels', as they are called), was a board-game called Gwenddoleu. On this the pieces moved about by themselves.

BRUIDNE

Translated as meaning 'hostels', the *bruidne* of ancient Ireland are depicted as centres of hospitality where all were welcome. A great cauldron maintained in each *bruiden* would feed everyone, no matter how many; feasting, drinking and general merriment were the order of the day.

The *bruidne* were, in fact, temples and mystical centres of certain ancient religions. The presence of the magical cauldron is evidence enough alone for this, the theme of such cauldrons being at the heart of many world religions. (Christians need look no further than their 'loaves and fishes' story for a parallel.) *Bruidne* tended· to be built 'over' or on both sides of streams. It is reported that they glowed with a great fire. This combination of fire and water is similar to that at the Persian Zoroastrian fire temples.

One of the great stories in Irish Mythology concerns the *Bruiden da Derga*, 'Da Derga's Hostel'. In this the 'hostel' is attacked and destroyed by invaders. . . but not before the attackers were confronted by several magical elements. The notion that such a story could be written about the mere sacking of a glorified pub is absurd. This was a religious conflict, doubtless between the old fire worshipping factions and newer ideas. (The site of Da Derga's 'Hostel' is close to the large modern 'youth hostel' in Co. Wicklow's Glencree. But there the similarity ends!)

C

CAISEAN UCHAD

A class of Celtic 'pass-the-parcel' ritual in which a sheep's head (set alight) was passed around a group of people. It was extremely bad luck to be left holding the head when the fire went out. The similarity to modern party games, such as 'pass-the-parcel', and 'musical chairs' is no coincidence. Games such as these which gradually eliminate people leaving one lucky or unlucky individual are remnants of ritualistic systems for picking rulers. . . or victims for sacrifice.

CÉNAD

A chant, sung through the fist by a magician; repeated, mantra-like, the singer entered a trance and then foretold the future. Holding one's hands in front of one's face to form an 'echo chamber' is the origin of the 'hands' position' used in prayer.

CHARTRES

A great druidic centre in Gaul, now France. Here the druids gathered in a conference in 70 AD and prophesied the eventual Celtic dominion of the world. Following almost immediately upon this the Celtic world went into nearly 2000 years of decline ! However, there is now some sign of recovery and it must be remembered that the Chartres conference gave no time scale.

CLIODHNA

Pronounced 'Clee-ona', this is a woman's name in modern Ireland, but, in earlier times, she was a supernatural female entity who lured young men away for sexual purposes. She was Banshee-like, in that she emitted a wail or call. This call was akin to that of sirens in Classical culture, and none could resist. She lived in the heart of rocks, but also near the sea. Connections have been drawn between her and the Gaulish 'Clutonda'. Cliodhna sometimes appears in the form of a wren. The Irish word for this bird has been translated as meaning 'Druid's Bird', maybe so. But in any event 'Wren Boys' were youths who hunted, captured and killed these birds. With branches decorated with their

(Cliodhna cont'd)

corpses they processed about, chanting ritually and demanding gifts of money and drink. The origination of this practice is from the custom of religious tax-gatherers in ancient times; bearing the symbol of their sacred animal, a wren, or pig, or whatever, and dressed in outlandish clothes to mystify and terrify the simple classes, the priestly castes moved around the countryside at particular important times of year. Christian 'Easter Dues' are a modest reminder of those times.

COSMOS

The notion of the world or universe as an orderly or systematic whole appears to have been central to our ancient religions; leaders both speculated upon the topic and ordered their affairs so as to conform to their conclusions. Thus came Ireland's ancient division into five provinces. These represented the four cardinal points plus a central core. The latter, now defunct, was known as the province of *Midhe*, which actually means 'middle' or 'centre'. The other ancient provinces are now represented by Ulster, Munster, Leinster, and Connacht. Within ancient *Midhe*, at the 'centre of the centre', so to speak, stood Tara. And the Court of Tara itself, it has been pointed out, was organised as a replica of the larger whole of the island. Parallels of this system of 'sacred centres' are found in all the great religions of the world.

COURSING

An unpleasant 'field sport' carried out in certain parts of Ireland. A wild hare, previously captured, is released into a fenced-off area, followed by specially trained greyhounds who chase after it. Sometimes they catch it and tear it to pieces; if it reaches a certain spot it is rescued by the organisers. . . and used again on another occasion. During its run away from the hounds the hare darts this way and that in its natural manner, only the fastest and most agile hound will catch it. The purpose of the whole exercise is to make money by both betting on a particular dog, and by increasing the value of dogs for the breeders. The origins of coursing are based on a system of divination used by the ancients. Before an important event, hares were released; the patterns of their running were carefully observed, and good or bad omens deduced. The Roman historian Dio Cassius tells us of such goings-on in Britain in the first century AD.

CROM CRUACH

An idol set up at Magh Slécht, 'Plain of Adoration', in County Cavan by the King,Tigernmas. Known as 'Lord of Death', Tigernmas is credited with the introduction of gold mining and of silverwork to Ireland. Some authorities have it that Tigernmas was a renegade Roman legion commander; this may be supported by the nature of the cult of Crom which has strong Eastern connections. Made of stone, Crom was sheeted in gold. Around him he had a circle of twelve little assistant idols, these sheeted in silver. Gods with twelve assistants or 'disciples' are of course of considerable antiquity, their number being linked to astrological systems. Crom is notable in that children ('first-born') were sacrificed to him at Samhain, amidst general mayhem and orgiastic activities. While Tigernmas himself was killed in one of these frenzies, his descendants are still with us in the form of the O'Conor family of Co. Roscommon who hold the title of O'Conor Don.

'Domnach Crom Dubh', (Black Crom's Sunday) is a day formerly celebrated, especially in the West of Ireland, by visits to particular wells and ancient sacred sites. Now Christianized, the most notable of these remaining pilgrimages is that to Croagh Patrick in Co. Mayo. The routines of this pilgrimage, traversing wilderness, climbing mountain, and ritualistic encircling of stones while chanting, all these survive from the days of Crom worship.

CRUACHÁN

The cave at Cruachan is the 'Entrance to The Otherworld' and regarded in the old religions as a place from which spirit forces and entities emerge. Caves such as this feature strongly in ancient beliefs but are generally nowadays ignored. An exception would be the modern Christian pilgrimage to Lough Derg in County Donegal, this pilgrimage originating in pre-Christian times as a visit to a cave where 'hell' could be examined. The Cruachan region of County Roscommon, modern-day Rathcroghan, is rich in locations associated with ancient magic, ritual and religion. The Rathcroghan mound itself is reputedly the remnants of the 'palace' of Queen Medb of Connacht. Whatever about that, it was used by rulers of that era as a place to consult magicians and sorcerers, particularly at the time of Samhain.

CRYSTAL GAZING

This was carried out to foretell events. Fedelm, a spirit in the form of a young blond woman wearing a green cloak, but perhaps a living priestess, gazed into a crystal on behalf of Queen Medb before the Táin, the great story of battle. Everything in the crystal was red !

CURSES

In different times man was much concerned with placing curses on his enemy, and avoiding those directed at himself ! A ritual, obviously evolved from earlier religious practices, developed. The old religions were very concerned with stones, their nature and their power *(see page 91)* and that concern gave rise to later folklore about the use of stones in both avoiding and casting curses. The 'Fire of Stones' curse is carried out in the following manner. Collect as many water-worn stones as would cover a family hearth. These, about the size of a fist, should be piled up into the shape of a fire. Then, with incantations (send £500 to the writer for details!) the curser places his/her curse on the enemy, the meantime praying that, until the heap of stones shall burn, the curse shall stay in place. The stones are then scattered in inaccessible places because, if the cursed one should gather them all together he may unravel the curse or worse, re-direct it at the other party. The combination of water, fire and stone in these rituals will remind us of the essence of the Old Religion.

While the Fire of Stones curse was carried out in private, there was also a system of public curses available. In certain locations there were, and indeed still are, types of altars with large fist shaped stones lying about on them. To curse one's enemy one went to these altars and 'turned' the stones. Literally, this involved turning the stones around three times on an anti-clockwise direction. Again, certain incantations to suitable entities were involved. In some locations these cursing stones were under the control of particular families. Only they could activate the curse on your behalf. For a contribution, of course ! This notion of a hereditary 'cursing class', a type of priesthood in fact, brings us back several thousand years. But not necessarily that long. On County Donegal's Tory Island in the last century the islanders were disturbed by the approach of a British gunboat, the Wasp, come to evict the tenants. The man responsible for such things activated the cursing stone of the island and the Wasp was wrecked, its crew drowned.

D

DAUGHTERS OF CALATIN

The 'triad' or concept of threeness is central to mankind's understanding of the spirit world. There are reasons for this. . . but they belong to another book. In any event, Christians will be as familiar with their Trinity as the ancients were with a ferocious threesome of female spirit entities, Badb, Macha, and Anand, daughters of Ernmas, associated with Queen Medb and Rathcroghan. In actuality this was the Triad Goddess of war. Sent away (to 'Babylon'?) by Medb, she recalled them to fight in the Táin.

DEAD

Victorian municipal graveyards marked the end for Christianity. Up to then people were buried round their churches and places of worship. The living prayed surrounded by their dead; they had a reason to visit Church every sunday, a psychic reason which had nothing to do with doctrine, rationale, or even with faith. It is part of us to visit our dead and there, in the presence of we-know-not-what, communicate with the world of Spirit. Once the huge hygienic cemeteries were constructed the link was broken; there was no reason to go to church anymore, no psychic *pull*, as it were.

This is the *real* reason Christianity lost its grip on the masses. The decline of religion has nothing to do with the Industrial Revolution or the rise of a better educated type of individual. Individuals nowadays are more sheep-like than ever, following the diktats of advertiser and lifestyle guru with slavish obedience. No. Christianity went into a nosedive of decline because of the construction of large cemeteries away from the churches. It has now petered out as a mass religion in the Western World.

Ancient man was very attached to ancestors. In Ireland a whole archaeological class of tomb ('court cairn') were constructed in such a manner as to accommodate ritual beside or, in fact, *inside* the ancestral graves. The nature of this ritual is obscure, but perhaps we may be guided by the practice of certain peoples in the present day world in

(Dead, cont'd)

'less developed' areas. These people, on a particular day, journey to their ancestral graves, take out the corpses or bones or whatever, dress them up in clothes, and party!

The concept of personal spiritual salvation or immortality was not as strongly developed in the ancients as with us. Their concern was more with the psychic cohesion of the tribe or group. Individual freedom is a luxury created by group effort. Paradoxically, the more successful the group is at creating the conditions for individual freedom, the sooner it collapses ! In the ancient scheme of things a person developing individuality was regarded as a threat to the leadership and promptly eliminated. 'Leadership' represented the spirit of the group and had to be protected. This concept developed into the 'Divine Right of Kings' of later eras.

Anciently then, the psychic cohesion of the group was its strength; this was a force that reached backwards in time through the ancestors, and stretched to the future through the young. Modern man does not have psychic cohesion. We have no graves, as such, and we slaughter millions of our children in the womb for our convenience. Essentially we are suffering from a psychic madness; this goes undiagnosed only because we enjoy the symptoms !

DIVINATION

All ancient spiritual systems were much concerned with this; those who knew (or claimed to know) the future were in control of the present. Modern societies are organised on similar lines, religions and political leaders largely basing their power on their supposed knowledge and/or control of the future.

The early Irish practised divination in many forms. Dreams were popular as a method. Those intending to tell the future prepared for a special sleep by eating particular meals, by sleeping in a particular manner, or by sleeping in a special location. Meals tended to be raw flesh. Falling asleep in the hide of a sacrificed animal was effective, as was sleeping on or tunnelled into a burial mound. Many of our tales tell of Heroes who were thus transported to the Otherworld.

The clouds were watched by a class of astrologer known as *néladoir,* *(see page 67),* their movements analysed. Others observed the flights of birds, and the presence of particular species. War or peace could be foretold in this way, life or death.

Sticks were cast by the druids and board games *(see page 67)* were played. Captured warriors were drained of blood, the blood watched as it filled a bowl. Sacrificial women were impaled on stakes, their contortions analysed for 'signs'. Crystals were examined, bowls of water stared into, and waves watched. All these methods were intrinsically absurd, their purpose being merely to (a) bedazzle the peasantry and (b) 'jolt' the diviner's mind into the psychic dimension necessary for future-telling.

DIVIZIACUS

A druid of the Euro-Celtic people the 'Aedui', Diviziacus visited Rome in 61 AD and met Cicero and his brother. They discussed details of Druidic doctrine. The modern equivalent of this meeting would be a visit from a a member of the Brazilian rain forest people to the Pope. Or to the Secretary-General of the UN. He would receive a polite and interested reception and then be shown the door. But not before a photo-opportunity to demonstrate to the world at large that the concerns of the rain forest folk were high on the agenda of affairs.

The actual details of 'Druidic doctrine' discussed are not easy to pin down. While Diviziacus no doubt spoke a type of Latin intelligible to Cicero, nonetheless the language required to express the Druidic concepts was not available.

DONN

The Dark One, Lord of The Dead. He lives on an island off the southwest coast of Ireland. Here we (the Irish) must go on our deaths. The actual island is unidentified. It may even be one of the Blaskets. Inisvickilaune ?

DUBLIN

It takes its name from Dubh, a word meaning 'black', but also the sorceress wife of Enna. Dubh killed Enna's other wife by magic; Enna in turn killed Dubh by drowning her in a pool in the River Liffey, hence *Dubh Linn*, Dubh's Pool. The city is the capital of Ireland and the only large city in the world under the absolute control of Celts.

E

EITHNE

The daughter of a King of Leinster. She was, as the custom, put into the care of foster-parents. It is recorded that those fosterers 'fed her with the flesh of children in order to make her the sooner ripe for matrimonial embraces'. This is an unusual reversal of 'normal' world-wide practices of ritual cannibalism. Generally this is used to slow down the ageing process, or to add strength. World folklore abounds with tales of elderly women draining the blood of virgins to drink in an effort to maintain youth. (Many of these elderly women are 'Count-esses', living in castles. Usually in Romania!) The modern cosmetic in-dustry keeps up this tradition; human placenta material is used in var-ious cosmetic concoctions.

Archaeological evidence in Ireland appears to confirm that, whatever about feeding on 'the flesh of children', the ancients were in the habit of splitting open bones to get at the marrow. Whether the bones were of slain enemies, or of admired deceased leaders, we cannot be sure. Certainly the practice was widespread in the ancient world, notably in ancient Egypt, where marrow was sucked out of bones for purposes mysterious.

END OF THE WORLD

Any culture worthy of the name has, in its mythology or protohistory, a story of a great battle, long and long ago, between Good and Evil. The Battle of Moytura is the Irish version. A struggle between Good and Evil, Light and Dark. The Tuatha dé Danaan, (regarded as the 'good') were the victors and afterwards their great Goddess celebrated victory by proclaiming it round Ireland. She told the hills, rivers, forests, and their spirits. Then, despite all this, she prophesied the end of time, and the rebirth of evil, and how it would overwhelm. In a later era the Druids echoed her. They saw the balance and the struggle and the tension between three mystical elements, Fire, Water, and Earth. In their scheme of things, Man and all his works were 'earth'. They put it simply. 'In the End', said the Druids, ' Fire and Water must one day prevail'.

ESANE

A mystical element released by magicians; the rite involved dropping hot coals into clear water. Those artificial hollows made in stones known as 'bullauns' are probably connected to this.

F

FARNBOG

These were the priests of Zarathustra in pre-Moslem Iran. Many early Irish religious practices and beliefs appear to have similarities with those in that country. Antiquarians of the 19th. Century put forward many theories about these apparent links. Such ideas are now unfashionable but the links remain: no-one, for example, has ever explained the origins of the word 'firbolg', the name of one of the peoples who came to Ireland in antiquity. While Bulga was the ancient God of Lightning, and 'Firbolg' could very well mean 'Men of the God of Lightning'; some say it derives from the Euro- Celts, the Belgae; others have it that it means 'bag-men', from a slave class of earth carriers with origins in Thrace. But could it really be *Farnbog* ?

FETH FIADA

A spell used by the Druids to create invisibility, particularly to appear as 'a mist'.

FOUNDATION SACRIFICE

When building a structure, it was the custom to offer a sacrifice to the earth to compensate for the affront caused by interference. A range of sacrifices were buried in the foundations. Humans, animals and precious objects were used. The remains of humans found in Ireland in such circumstances appear to be middle-aged males. The animals were usually horses. In latter days, the last few centuries, horses' heads were regularly buried under a flagstone in front of the fire of a house being built. This was supposedly done to 'improve the echo' of dancers' feet, but obviously was a continuation of the earlier custom. Ritual outlives belief! And the ritual continues to modern times with the practice of burying valuable items in the foundations of important public buildings.

G

GABHA-BHEIL

'The Trial by Bel', a ritual in which innocence or guilt was judged by an accused's ability to walk over a fire three times. Bel is a God associated both with death and fire; his feast is *Bealtaine* (1st of May).

GEIS

A form of obligation or personal taboo imposed upon certain individuals. A *geis* was imposed either by druids or by individuals with close psychic relationships with the other. To break a *geis* inevitably meant death. Many *geasa* were arbitrary or absurd, though some arose logically from aspects of the personal history or background of the individual concerned. Conaire Mór, whose father was a bird, was thus under obligation not to kill them. In fact it may very well be that all *geasa* had origins in animal totem/taboo systems. Fionn Mac Cumhaill (whose dogs were the offspring of his sister!) was constrained from eating that animal. The complications of mythological stories frequently arises because of the efforts of individuals to avoid breaking their *geis*.

GUATAVITA

The name of a lake in Colombia (South America) where, up to the 17th Century, the Muisca Indians organised a ceremony involving the casting of precious objects into the depths. Loughnashade is a lake in Co. Armagh, close to and associated with Eamhain Macha, one of the major centres of ancient Ireland and capital of Ulster in the historical times. Loughnashade may be translated as 'Lake of the Jewels' or 'Precious Lake'. Bones and musical instruments have been found under its waters. The 'Loughnashade Trumpet' is in Dublin's National Museum. A lake of almost identical name, with similar meaning, Shad Lough is situated close to Rathcroghan in Co. Roscommon. This location was another major centre of ancient Ireland and was capital of Connacht up to early Christian times. We draw what conclusions that we may from such strange connections.

H

HARES

Priestesses kept a hare in their bodice. These tamed creatures would be released and watched for auguries. This custom gave rise in later years to several absurd notions. Many believed that 'witches' could actually turn into hares. A man in Scotland, accused of murdering a woman in the 18th century, protested that when he had hit her with a spade she had actually been in the form of a hare. (The judge didn't believe him either, and he was hanged!) Similarly, many thought that 'witches' were in the habit of suckling the devil, he appearing for nourishment in the form of an animal. Women with a third nipple (of whom statistically there are nowadays one in two hundred) were thought to be definite witches, the extra nipple being for the devil. Hares were, of course, sacred animals even in Egypt, there they worshipped a hare-headed divinity. In Ireland hares would not be eaten and could only be hunted on *Bealtaine,* or May Day. An example of how folklore travels in circles is the belief that witches, in the form of hares, suckled at cows, taking the best milk. This is related to the notion that the devil, in the form of a hare, suckles at women who are witches. Also, it's bad luck to mention the very word 'hare'. . .on a boat. . .in Scotland.

HOLY FAMILY

The pre-Christian Celtic religion had a parallel to the 'Holy Family' of Christianity. In the Celtic scheme there was a triadic family of Father God, Mother God, and Divine Son. Outside Ireland these were known as Teyrnon, Matrona, and Mabon. Mabon was known as Maponus in Northern Britain and in Gaul. The 'Cult of Maponus' was well known, he was strongly associated with Holy Wells. His mother was (perhaps naturally enough) a river. This Matrona is the River Marne in France. And in Ireland, where Matrona is called Boand, she is the River Boyne. The Father God here is The Daghda and the Divine Son is Aenghus. The dwelling of Aenghus (regarded also as the God of Love) is Newgrange, now popular with tourists.

I

IMBAS FOROSNA

A divination ritual, perhaps to be translated as 'illumination between the hands'. The diviner first chewed raw flesh, then incanted over his/her hands and placed the hands over the cheeks. The hidden is thus revealed; perhaps through no more complex a cause than indigestion, much as modern man, after eating pork or whatever, experiences vivid dreams of occult quality.

IMPALEMENT

This was a favoured method of Celtic human sacrifice. Particularly recorded in the case of high-born women captives, these being 'skewered lengthwise' and left as gifts to the goddess Anu. Their screaming was intended to attract the Goddess. The Celtic rite of Taghairm is connected to this. In Taghairm black cats were impaled and roasted on fires. Their horrendous screeching would attract other cats and, eventually, a great cat-like creature, the 'cat-spirit' would appear. This entity would grant favours. (This activity is associated with the mysterious Scottish phrase 'Giving his supper to the devil'.)

Modern Irish hooligans regularly throw live cats into fires at Hallowe'en, thus answering unconsciously the call of some primaeval instinct. As yet, in modern times, only psychotics and film makers are involved with the impalement of women. A sobering realization is that many of the activities of present-day psychotics were perfectly respectable institutional activities of the ancients; ritual cannibalism, torture and mutilation being commonplace occurences. The psychotic tends to echo the past in his or her behaviour.

INSANITY

The remedy for this condition was the burial of a live cock. Burial of living creatures was regarded as useful for various purposes. Live men were buried under dwellings to placate the earth for disturbance. Live women were buried in fields for productivity.

L

LEPRECHAUN

Apart from the word 'bomb', the word 'leprechaun' is probably the one most associated with Ireland throughout the world. Close behind come the words 'fairy' and 'banshee'. Everyone thinks they know what these mean, few do.

Some rule of existence seems to determine that the most important mysteries of a culture are translated into the most ludicrous concepts when that culture is superceded. It is as if the new culture realizes that some things just cannot be extirpated. But they can be controlled by diminishing them as concepts and integrating them into the new schema.

Lugh is the great Sun God of the Irish, patron of Arts and Crafts, leader of the Tuatha dé Danaan. And not only of the Irish, he is God of the Euro-Celts; European cities such as London, Léon, Loudan, Lyons, Laon, Liegnitz, Leiden and Carlisle all owe their names to Lugh. And beyond the Celts in time and geography, Lugh (known as *Lugh Lamhfada*, 'long-armed Lugh') is rooted in the Indo-European pantheon of Gods. To a believer (if there were a believer !) Lugh would be as important as Christ is to a Christian. Instead he is now a 'leprechaun'. A little character with buckled shoes, green hat, and tweed waistcoat. He sometimes sits on toadstools. And in his vicinity there are frequently other little people with pointed hats (and pointed ears). The male variety are cute-eyed, mischievous, but nice. Like a guy a girl would hope to meet at a Fleadh Ceoil. Except a lot smaller. The female variety of these fairies (for these are them) is invariably pretty. And wears a First Holy Communion Dress. These 'little people' dance a lot. They say things like "come away o human child, to the waters and the wild, with a fairy hand in hand, for the world's more full of weeping, than you can understand". Great poetry like this is no bother to them. And why would it be ? For these 'fairies' are the Tuatha dé Danaan. The people of the Goddess Anu. These are the people of Light, the Rulers, the Gods and Goddesses of Ancient Ireland. When driven out and dispossessed by newcomers (well us, actually, the Gaels) the Tuatha took to the hills. Or, more precisely, *into* them. And absolutely precisely, into the burial mounds of peoples even more ancient. There they carry on a parallel existence. In former times they were real enough, emerging in human enough form to have sex with us (the Gaels) or to slaughter us. Or to do both. Over the last few centuries they have shrunk considerably, however. Much too small to slaughter us, let alone have sex, they get up to mischief instead. Turning milk sour. Hiding things. Nothing serious. Just bad-neighbour behaviour. The serious stuff is left to a singular character, the Banshee. She sits up in a tree. Wearing white, she sits there on a dead branch, combing her hair. . . and wailing. Be assured that you do not want to hear her. If you hear the banshee, you or one of yours will surely shortly die. The Banshee is The Real Thing. Her name is derived from the Irish 'Fairy Woman'. Sometimes a hag, other times a beautiful woman, the Banshee is at the heart of ancient spirituality. Her ability to appear as hag or beauty is that of the Cailleach, that 'hag' character who, when embraced by a Hero, will turn into a beauty. In essence that Cailleach is the Spirit of Ireland. Getting old and weary . . . to be revived by a new champion. Inevitably he will fail her. But someone else will come along. She lives forever. This is quite reassuring until we notice that in certain parts of Ireland this banshee/cailleach character is still called 'The Badb'. In modern Irish the word means a 'dangerous frightening being of the female sex'. Badb is the War Goddess. In old stories she appears, sometimes as a crow (hence that old woman sitting in the tree), but other times as a naked screaming female entity in battlefields. As late as the Battle of Clontarf (1014AD) she appeared, a shrieking crow over the heads of the warriors. Badb is actually part of the great triad Goddess of old. Another name for her is Anu.

We've killed off Lugh, of Light, and of Art and Craft. We've made him a leprechaun. We've relegated most of the Tuatha dé Danaan to the role of silly fairies. In our inherited spirit world we have really nothing much left. Except for the 'death' aspect of the great Goddess, the part of her concerned with war, and battle, continuous strife. We read about her every day in the newspapers.

M
MUSIC

Bronze janglers, trumpets, bone pipes and stringed lyres appear to have been involved in early music which itself was always associated with dance. Celtic funerary rites involved music and naked dancing girls. Supposedly 'traditional' instruments such as harp or bagpipes are fairly recent introductions, the harp first mentioned only in the ninth century AD, while the bagpipes are mediaeval. Anyone who aspired to being a leader in ancient Ireland was required to be accomplished in Arts, and particularly in music.

MUR OLLAVAN

The City of the Learned, a drudic college of around 927 BC.

NIGHT AND DAY

In early Ireland the night was regarded as preceeding the day. Calendars and calculations of dates, feasts, festivals and anniversaries reckoned the event to start with the fall of night and continue until the following sunset. There is strong mystical significance in all this, quite apart from the fact that to consider life as a series of periods where light follows dark seems to portray a healthy optimism.

Modern man does most of his human things at night. Makes love, gets drunk, meets friends. We regard these activities as coming *after* the events of the day, events such as working in office or factory or spreading slurry or whatever. Coming *after*, the human events are relegated in importance and we have less energy anyway to carry them out. The ancients sensibly *started* each period by making love, getting drunk, and meeting friends. They then put any remaining energy into work, war and other ecologically negative activities. On the mystical level, the acceptance that darkness was the primary condition and the parallel understanding that light was merely an accident of the cosmos gave our ancestors a depth of natural understanding that does not come easy to ourselves. In light we see illusion. In darkness we have advance notice of what it will be like when our eyes are shut forever. This gives us time to prepare ourselves. End of sermon.

NINE TO FIVE

The sacred number of the Irish is *nine*, just as seven is that of Eastern societies. The Celts had a *nine* day week in earlier times. In the mythological stories *nine* re-occurs. Cuchulainn had *nine* weapons. Medb had *nine* chariots. Niall had *nine* hostages. The number *five* is also important. There are *five* provinces. There are *five* major roads, and *five* hostels. Both the residents of the Otherworld and Fionn Mac Cumhaill are regarded as counting in *fives*. The number *five* is associated with 'power'.

ONAN

A Biblical character who got in trouble for 'spilling his seed upon the ground'. Generations of adolescent males have been taught that this was an example of God's dislike of masturbation but in actuality it perhaps has more to do with the pagan kingship rites of antiquity. In these the claimant to kingship 'married' the earth and carried out certain rituals to consummate the marriage. In Ireland this was known as *banaisrighe*. Certain specified spots in Ireland were designated for this rite. In Connacht, for example, *banaisrighe* was carried out at Carnfree in County Roscommon. Certain hereditary roles of assistant to the new king at the ceremony, of gatekeeper to keep out the curious whilst the ceremony took place, and so forth, were held by particular families. The Spirit of the Earth in Connacht was, in fact, Medb, now known as a human 'Queen Maeve'; her record for promiscuity arises from the numbers of rival claimants to the kingship. The name of Medb, perhaps not incidentally, is translated as 'the intoxicating one'.

PERSONALITY

"When they meet together they converse with few words and in riddles, hinting darkly at things for the most part and using one word when they mean another; and they like to talk in superlatives, to the end that they may extol themselves and depreciate all other men. They are also boasters and threateners and are fond of pompous language, and yet they have sharp wits and are not without cleverness at learning." These words were not written yesterday, after a visit to an Irish pub by a foreign observer. But many will feel they could have been. No, these are the observations of old Diodorus Siculus of the first century BC. The personality of a race would appear to survive over enormous periods of time. Why is this ?

PHYSICIANS

The Irish word for such is *'Lia'*. Essentially meaning 'cures', this originally would have come from a phrase meaning 'Professor of Cures'. However, Lia also means 'a pillar-stone'. So a physician might just as well have been a 'Professor of Pillar-Stones'. Stones were, of course, used for healing purposes. Incidentally, in Scots Gaelic *Lia* also means a pig. The *Lia Fail* is a celebrated stone, of which there are two claiments to the title which means ' stone of destiny'. (This could equally be translated as the Pig of Destiny!) One claimant to the title stands at Tara, the other lies beneath the Coronation Throne of British sovereigns in Westminster Abbey. On occasion it is kidnapped by Scottish Nationalists. The Irish version was reputed to 'roar' when a rightful ruler stood on it. The London edition, with typical British skilful diplomacy, remains silent for all rulers, right or wrong.

PIGS

The mystical significance of these animals is a major theme in the concerns of Ancient Ireland. Giant pigs wandered the countryside, laying waste to all around. It fell to heroes to kill these animals. Other pigs had the ability, after having been slaughtered and eaten, to re-appear the next day. In modern Ireland there are numerous names of-places associated with pigs. The Muclaghs in County Roscommon (*Muc* being the Irish for pig) are huge earthworks of great antiquity, and of mysterious function or purpose. Muclagh is also the name of a townland in County Wicklow. The Black Pig's Grave is in Enniscrone, County Sligo. The Black Pig's Dyke is yet another structure. A ritual ceremony occurred in County Cork up to the early 1800's. This, on Samhain Eve, involved a horde of youths wandering the countryside in bizarre costumes, demanding contributions for the Muc-Olla. Farmers who refused were apt to suffer damages, it was thus an early form of trick-or-treat.

So what is all this about ? The pig, as an animal, would not appear to have many intrinsic 'mystical' characteristics. Our modern pig is fairly ordinary and the pig of the ancients appears to have been equally mundane. Though savage with it ! No, the pig's power over man lies in its association with the Firbolg, one of the races of ancient Ireland. As in Britain, where there were 'Cats of War' and 'Cow People' and so forth, peoples in Ireland were known by their own sacred animal or totem. It may be relevant to remember that peoples in antiquity were named by their neighbours.

PLACE

The magic and ritual associated with *place* are largely lost to modern man. Carrying an overburden of *ideas* wherever we travel, the more subtle and less raucous psychic rhythyms of individual places are blanked out from our consciousness. Only certain locations with particular powerful psychic emissions affect us. To the ancients it was different. The average individual then didn't know very much. Without knowledge it is difficult to formulate ideas so the reliance was more on feelings and instinct. The ancients found it easy to 'tune in' to the vibrations of place. *Dindshenchas*, meaning the Lore of (famous) Places, is an important branch of learned tradition. Virtually every feature of landscape has mythic significance; the land itself had a spiritual entity which was not entirely separate from the consciousness of its inhabitants. Interestingly, the ' sanctuaries ' or holy places of the Celtic ancients were set up both on territorial boundaries and at the core. These places of psychic power were set up both to protect the integrity of the territory and warn anyone who might contemplate incursion.contemplate ncursion.

R

REEL

A Celtic dance, common to Ireland and Scotland. Its clockwise circular movements originated in sun-worship. Moving thus in the same direction of the sun is regarded as auspicious. Followers of Islamic Sufism and particularly of the teachings of the poet Rumi, (known as 'whirling dervishes' to Victorian observers), spin round like tops, clockwise. Wine moves round modern elegant tables in similar fashion, a practice which, as Poseidonius tells us, dates from Celtic antiquity.

REINCARNATION

An essential aspect of belief in this phenomenon in ancient Ireland appears to be the reappearance of one's ancestors as one's descendants. Thus, while the individual him/herself was not necessarily a reincarnation, she/he formed a link between past and future. This is very subtle. Perhaps less so is the story of Tuan Mac Carell whose existence (as he said) went from boar to eagle, to warrior to salmon. As a salmon he was eaten and conceived by his mother as a human.

ROTH FAIL

Translated either as 'Wheel of Light' or 'Wheel of Destiny', this was understood to be a device or machine used by the druids to travel through space. A pillarstone in Co. Tipperary, *Cnamhcoill* Stone, was regarded as a remnant of this machine. The *Peithynes* or Druid's Wheel of Wales was a spinning/flickering thing with some affinity to the *Roth Fail*. All these were no doubt devices used to create altered consciousness. Disco lighting and those banks of video screens in retail outlets are modern examples of *roth fail*. It is noted that these are used to *control* rather than to *liberate* the human spirit. This is an example of a common occurence wherby one culture subverts the magic/ritual of another and adapts it to its own use; usually creating a meaning in direct opposition to the original.

RAIN MAKING

When struck with drought, the young women of an area got together and, selecting one of their virginal number, stripped her of her clothes and, carrying her aloft, dumped her in a well. This custom was carried out until mediaeval times. Then, however, she was merely dunked and fished out again. In antiquity she was a sacrifice. Virginity was a very dangerous state in antiquity. It is recorded that groups of women, devotees of the Goddess, would gather once a year and, selecting one of their number, tear her limb from limb. Then, armed with an arm, or a leg, a thigh, or foot or whatever, they would rush about in a frenzy, alarming people.

S

SACRED FIRE

Takht-i-Saliman in Persia was where the sacred fire called Atur Gushnasp burned 'forever'. Or it did, at least, until the Muslims put it out! Kildare in Ireland was where the sacred fire of Brigit burned, equally forever. Until the Christian Normans put *it* out. Sacred fires are particularly vulnerable to unbelievers with buckets of water but, nonetheless, they commonly existed throughout antiquity. Numerous sites in Ireland had perpetual fires, Brigit's Kildare fire being merely one of them. Brigit was a Goddess, a patron of poets. She is connected to the Brigindo of the Gauls and the Brigantia in Britain. In Ireland her fires were tended by the *'Inghea Andagha'*, daughters of fire. Her festival is *Imbolc*, the First of February. This is associated with lactation. Brigit's fire was tended by virgins. Christianised later, these virgins became nuns, and one of these nuns became the Christian saint Brigid. The sacred fire actually lasted long into the Christian era. That little red light kept burning constantly in modern Catholic churches is its glimmer.

In a sense, of course, all fires in ancient times were sacred, fire itself being a phenomenon to be tended and worshipped. In Ireland there was much ritual connected to fire, most pervasively perhaps the notion that on a certain date all fires were extinguished and then re-lit from a central 'sacred' fire ignited by the priestly classes. St Patrick's lighting of 'Paschal' fires was of course a fairly crude but successful effort to muscle in on this ritual. *Bealtaine* (the First of May) was the time of year when Druids re-lit the fires. In Christian times up to the 19th Century the ordinary people would wait until smoke came out of the priest's chimney before lighting up on this date.

SHAMROCK

The original 'shamrock' was actually water cress. This was regarded as having sacred and magical qualities. Whereas modern watercress sandwiches are regarded as terribly polite, redolent of English vicarage gardens, in earlier times the plant appears to have been a female aphrodisiac. In any event those eating cress/shamrock gained the power to 'see fairies'. Modern shamrock is a type of clover. Shamrock-like plants are 'special' to all Celtic cultures. The *fleur-de-lis* of France is a heavily stylised *(naturellement !)* shamrock.

SILENCE OF THE LAMBS

In mythology Aoife was the lover of Ilbrec who was the son of the Sea-God, Manannán mac Lir. Aoife was skinned, the skin being made into a bag which the Fianna used to carry around their 'treasure' or sacred and symbolic objects. When killed, Aoife was in the form of a crane bird, to which she had been turned. These birds are regarded as good luck omens; departing the countryside in times of war, their presence thus implies that peace will prevail.

A relationship between women and birds, and the interconnection between them and religious belief and practice, these are constant themes in many world cultures. The origins of this are obscure. Spacemen have been suggested. But whatever. The story of Aoife brings us across the Atlantic to South American cultures. Here, in Mexico, Huitzilopochtli was a War-God, also having dominion over the weather and the crops. He was depicted partially feathered. In a particular ceremony a woman was selected as symbolic mother to the God. This victim's skin was removed in a large cloak-like piece which the officiating priest would don. Prancing about in a ritual fashion, the male priest would thus appear to the mob below as a woman, the breasts of the sacrificed bouncing on his chest and so forth. Allied to this, the priest was also decorated with feathers of large birds, large crane-like birds. The combination of feathers and female form would doubtless have had a profound effect upon the public.

A modern American movie called *Silence of The Lambs* has also had a profound effect upon the public. This features a psychotic transvestite character who dresses up in women's skin, rather than in their clothes. While a mob of thousands watched the Huitzilopochtli ceremonies. . . a mob of tens of millions have watched our modern movie equivalent. What does all this mean ? What is the difference between these ceremonies ? Granted, the actresses in the movie went home afterwards in their Porches, as distinct from their long-ago South American sisters. But is a ritual where we only *pretend* to sacrifice a victim any different than the real thing ? Why bother with the ritual at all, what is the *point* ? To all these questions there may very well be answers. And one that occurs is that movies are essentially the ritual of modern mass-religion. And the screen, in cinema or living room, this is a type of altar. Here are safely acted out the sacrificial dramas of the ancients.Though that scarcely answers the question, what is the *point* ? What is the *point* of sacrifice, whether it be bread and wine, or virgin, son-of-God, or ox, goat, sheep or pig. . .what is the *point* ?

SLINNEIREACHAD

This was 'divination by shoulder-blade'. The right blade bone of a black pig or sheep was stripped of flesh and examined. A practice of the greatest antiquity, this occured in many cultures and is mentioned in the Bible.

SNAKES

There are no snakes in Ireland. Saint Patrick drove them out. Everyone knows this. Less generally known is that Saint Cado of Brittany is credited with driving snakes out of Gaul, while a similar feat was performed by Doué de Gozon in Malta. Whether there are snakes in 'Gaul' or Malta now is neither here nor there; the story has nothing to do with the presence or absence of real live slithery snakes but is a reminder of ancient serpent worship. Despite the absence of real snakes in Ireland there are no shortage of representations. Many of these are, of course, in religious art and the snakes appear being crushed, squashed or otherwise having a bad time at the feet of Saint Patrick. Others are peculiar, to say the least. What are we to make of the image of a woman whose legs are snakes ? Or of a snake emerging from a vagina ? Are these connected to that Euro-Goddess depicted with snakes around her legs ? Or to the Abraxis of the Christian gnostics ? Why are modern women fascinated by snakes ? What about the great 'worm' reported to haunt the bottom of lakes ? And Saint Michael and the dragon, where is the connection between this and those rocky islands around the coast associated with the same saint ? Why is the writer asking these questions ?

STAB IN THE BACK

Sacrificial victims were stabbed in the back. Their death convulsions were examined for signs. Other victims were stabbed in the front, their entrails were then examined.

Obviously any species that stabs sacrificial victims in the back (or the front) has not reached its full spiritual potential. But there we are. The mere fact that human hand and metal knife co-exist in the material world ensures that at some point or other a back will be stabbed. To establish man's position, the state of his holistic development at any one point in history, we must work on a ratio basis, rather than that of mere incident. What percentage of backs are stabbed, in one culture, as distinct from another culture ? For example, in our culture, among young male blacks in New York City the percentage is very high, though the stab in the back has technologically been superceded by the Uzi machine gun bullet in the chest.

What percentage of Kurds are bombed by napalm/poison gas, as distinct from the percentage slaughtered in former years by swords? Or even compared to the percentage clubbed to death in ancient times ? We will find that the percentage is rising. Just as with the young blacks in New York City, their ancestors were far safer in West Africa in proportion to their numbers. So what can we infer from this ? Lots of things. But chiefly that life is gettting more dangerous.

Why is life getting more dangerous ? There can only be three things responsible for increasing danger. Bad people. Bad systems. And natural disaster. We can leave out the natural disaster, which is just around the corner and in fact is not 'natural' but the result of bad people operating bad systems. The forthcoming ecological catastrophe will make all our speculations irrelevant.

But still it would be nice to know, *why* ? (As the sacrificial victim might well have asked!). *Why* is this happening, *why* are there so many bad people and bad systems ? The answer of the ancients was that there were forces and Gods of Good and Evil, in continual tension, and sometimes one was in the ascendant, sometimes another. But what did the ancients know ? They didn't even have television.

STONES

Large stones (megaliths) either standing alone, or as part of circles and alignments, or as part of tombs or other constructions, these are the most accessible of monuments of ancient Ireland. And the most baffling to the modern mind. We are used to structures of one sort or another, we continually build for many functions and purposes and our buildings take on many architectural and engineering forms. Consequently our immediate response to the megaliths of the ancients is to see them as akin to our own constructions and to use the same cultural vocabulary for their analysis. Thus we decide, for example, that a stone circle is an observatory. Or, in another view, that it is a 'temple of worship'. All discussion is then based on the arguments for or against these points of view. A leap of imagination is required to break free from this pattern of thinking.

(Stones, cont'd)

However, before that leap is taken, many get bogged down in techni-calities and queries. Perhaps understandably. The whole business of stones is highly complex. In certain parts of Ireland the stones are so high, elsewhere they are consistently higher. Some circles have an alignment, others an entranceway, or again, a flat altar-like stone. Some circles are not circles at all, being merely the remaining kerb stones of vanished burial mounds. In contrast to all this the single 'standing stones' are simple. Or they should be. But do they mark boundaries or routes, are they memorials of grave or of battle ? Or are they what archaeologists call 'cult stones' ?

'Cult Stone' is a phrase very popular among archaeologists. In fact the word 'cult' itself is attached to anything that cannot be understood through pollen analysis or dendrochronology. 'Possible cult stone' is a useful phrase too, leaving open a getaway to academic respectability in case of further discovery. Modern archaeology is a science in a similar state to that of physics thirty years ago. Then, physicists knew everything. Shortly afterwards, however, they learned a few more things and now realise that they know nothing and are, to borrow a phrase, eating soup with a fork. In fact, if it were raining soup, ar-chaeologists would be out in the fields with forks. But soon they will discover the spoon. Just as they have recently discovered sex.

Phallic is a word that pops up a lot these days. Round topped stones have been called 'male', flat-topped ones 'female'. In Ulster these male and female stones are found in pairs, like married couples. *La Tene* decoration represents, it is said, the 'swirl of semen'. A hole in a stone is a dead giveaway. And don't let's start on *Sile na Gigs*. . .The only explanation for this school of archaeology is that its distinguished practitioners are also men of a certain age surrounded by nubile girl students. But perhaps that is the explanation for most things !

Whatever about cults and sex , of course a stone circle is an 'observatory'. But only in the sense that a Christian church, aligned to the East, is a device for working out the points of the compass. And likewise a circle is a 'temple'. . . though merely in that vague but complex sense in which many of our modern buildings are temples. In a doctor's surgery we *hope* to learn that we may be cured. In a supermarket we *dream* of finding interesting nourishment at a reasonable cost. In an Art Gallery we *expect* to have our senses exercised. And so on. All structures are in this sense temples, all walls absorb our thoughts. Our hopes and dreams and expectations are in them. And not only *our* hopes and dreams and expectations, but the hopes and dreams and expectations of those who have gone before us, those who have visited these buildings in the past.

Behind us we all leave reflections of our psychic presence and, up to recently, our buildings have had a resonance relevant to their function. A shop *felt* like a shop. A factory, like a factory. A dwelling like a dwelling and so on. Up to recently. In the immediate past buildings have tended to become physically the same but, more significantly, buildings have become *newer*. Modern Western Man spends a lot of time in *new* buildings. A five or ten or even twenty year old building has had no time to acquire a satisfying aura of its own. We sleep in them, work in them, pray in them, but our activities receive no feedback, no spiritual confirmation.

All this is known. Known not in the sense that it is written down and analysed, but known in the sense that in recent years Modern Western Man has started to prefer old buildings to new. The elites of our societies now sleep in *old* houses. Fashionable professionals now work in *old* buildings. The most expensive shops are situated in converted warehouses and the like, *old* structures. Nice restaurants are decorated with *old* bricks, *old* beams and *old* bric-a-brac. Macdonalds hamburger restaurants, totally missing the point, are decorated with plastic imitations of *old* things. But Macdonalds don't have an adviser on psychic auras in their hamburger university. One day, they will.

Churches are perhaps the oldest buildings that remain in use. In many communities the church is, perhaps, the only building over fifty years old still in use for its original function. In Ireland many church structures are hundreds of years old. And even with that, in relationship to the spiritual history of their sites the buildings are merely newcomers. The site came first, recognised by the ancients for some spiritual quality which we have no method to analyse. The actual site is far more important than any old remaining stones or structures. A great number of Irish towns and villages are, it is worth remembering, situated where they are for no reason of trade or topography, but simply because some forgotten ancient pagan site became site of church or monastery and the settlement grew up around.

'Pagan' does not denote a short period before the introduction of Christianity. For fifteen hundred years or so we have been Christians. But for two thousand years before we were one sort of pagan, and two

(Stones, cont'd)

thousand years before that another brand of pagan. . . and for the next two thousand years ? Probably yet another variety !

But as to the structures on the sacred sites. Great earth mounds, stone cairns or megalithic structures were built for purposes mysterious. We know what some of them were used for, at some stage in their history, but such uses in many cases were totally at variance with their original purpose.   Much in the manner that modern redundant churches are used for discount carpet warehouses, a function for which they are ideally suited, the ancient structures went through similar transformations. And much as commonsense tells us that the church-warehouse wasn't actually built as such, commonsense also tells us that the ancient structures had some previous function. However, in the case of modern buildings we vaguely remember the original function of a church . . . with the ancient structures we have no such memory. And no amount of scholarly research will jog that memory. There is no route back. We have to move *forward* in our consciousness to rediscover the understandings of the past. This movement requires that leap of imagination mentioned above.

And what is the point of all this discussion in relationship to *stones* ? Let's think small for a moment. Stone circles, standing stones and megalithic tombs are huge and awesome structures, their very size perhaps preventing understanding. We are dominated by these and often forget that the ancients also made use of stone on a smaller scale. In burials sometimes are found little collections of bead like stones. What was their use ?   Carried around by obviously important individuals and buried with them, were these akin to the crystals of Californian culture ? Or were they 'badges of office' similar perhaps to the large crucifix worn by Christian bishops ? Or did they have a practical use akin to Arab 'worry beads' or Catholicism's rosaries ? Counters or calculators. . .in several parts of Ireland there are mysterious patterns of grooves cut out of rock . . . could these little pebble stones have been used for rolling round in these grooves as astronomical calculators ? Was thus their original purpose 'scientific' and then, in later eras, the science forgotten, did they take on mystical significance ? Do we have a link here to the 'turning' or 'cursing' stones of folklore ?

A lot of questions seem to arise. Perhaps it would be better to turn from the complexities of small stones and big circles and sacred sites to the quietness of tombs. Unlike circles, of mysterious function, truly we can say that the characteristic dolmens (beloved of the postcard industry) are definitely the remains of tombs. But merely the remains. Formerly covered with mounds of earth or rubble, what we see to-day is the internal skeleton of the structure. Why ? Why did the ancients use such huge stones, performing no decorative or monumental function, just to be hidden away ? Grossly inconvenient to people with no 'technology', what was the purpose in using these monstrous boulders ? Admittedly there are those who believe that the stones were no problem to the ancients because they were in possession of a type of psychokinetic power whereby huge objects could be moved at will. (Anyone who believes this, stop reading now !). For those that remain, a few more questions. Why were stone circles made out of stone ? This was wooded country. Why not mark out an 'observatory' or 'temple' with great logs ? Stone is certainly more permanent. . . but that is an argument that could be applied to modern telegraph poles. Why don't we use stone telegraph poles ? Because it would be ridiculous, that's the simple answer. Granted, our timber poles rot through every so many years but we accept that, replacing them with new ones. Made of timber, naturally. Man's inbuilt sense of cost benefit analysis tells him that, compared to the trouble of replacing timber every thirty years or so, the sheer trouble of erecting permanent stone telegraph poles is just not on.

There is no reason to believe that early man did not also possess this quality or ability to behave in an effective manner. Stone circles to him would be ridiculous, as would the use of huge hidden stones in tombs. Stone marker posts equally, why bother ? Why bother unless there was some inherent quality in the stone itself, something necessary for the function of the structure. Why should modern man bother using copper in electrical components ? An expensive metal, there are many cheaper available. Yes, but everyone knows that copper conducts electricity most effectively. And stone ? Likewise. The ancients knew that it conducted and stored a particular form of energy. And a *different* form of energy than that conducted and stored by trees or logs; it is recorded that the ancient Israelites had both sacred stones *and* sacred trees, with differing functions. Aaron's problems with the golden calf are connected to all this. But that's a long story.

Back to the future. And imagine a future world where electricity no longer exists, where the very word is forgotten. What might our descendants make of the ruins of power stations that they find

(Stones, cont'd)

beneath the desert sands ? Our descendants, who will doubtless be ragged bands of earth-worshipping nomads, will have no cultural vocabulary to analyse our power stations. All technology anyway may well be taboo to them. Their role in time will be to move the world back to health after our depredations. They will stare at power stations, shake their heads and say, "some ancient cult. . . God Our Mother only knows what they believed". And go about their business. This is how we behave. Our society and science is based on ignoring whole sections of human wisdom and experience, equally of the past and the present. Individuals who think and behave differently are categorised as something apart. Some we give the Nobel Prize. Others we label as cranks. The gap between Nobel prizewinner and crank is very very slim, a matter of fashion. (And it gets slimmer by the year !) This categorization in our society is of course its strength. The great thrust of materialism can crash on while individuals and groups within in do their own thing, believe their own beliefs. Up to a point. The majority would still prefer to have their appendix removed by the graduate of a good medical school than by an expert in out-of-body experience. Man is a commonsense animal. But with infinite capacity for self delusion.

But self-delusion is very useful. Absurd ideas are vital. Man thinks in the same way that evolution acts; evolution throws up all sorts of varieties of life in the belief that some of them will prove viable, and man gets all sorts of brilliant ideas in a similar expectation. From the pool of brilliant and absurd ideas we pick our futures. It is as if we know that logic doesn't work, that we can only learn something new by being illogical and daft. The absurd leads to knowledge.

Remember 'Pet Rocks' ? A vogue, a craze, a silly joke. People (mostly in Manhattan) kept little rocks in cardboard kennels.   Everyone laughed merrily for a while and then got absolutely bored rigid by the notion.   It went away.   And re-emerged some years later as. . . Crystals.   Serious stuff in California.   Books, industries, experts. Crystals, it is said, conduct and store a particular energy. Different crystals have different properties and each individual should be examined to discover which crystal is applicable to their individual requirements. This will cost you. But that's life. And folks with crystals in their pockets will get what were formerly known as 'good vibes'. Good vibes ? Never mind that the same folks are wearing sandals made by slave labour in Thailand. Never mind the bad vibes from the sandals. Crystals as a concept are way up there in comparison to 'Pet Rocks'. The crystal concept is *vaguely* connected to the reality of the ancient religions. But let's not get carried away. Consider for a moment an alien from Alpha Centauri (whom I know many of my readers meet on a daily basis but . . .) This alien, arriving on earth, might very well believe that the essence of Christianity is to nail people to crosses, rather than to love the neighbour as thyself. The alien mightn't understand 'love', whereas nailing people to crosses is sort of a universal concept !

We are all aliens when visiting the past. The wrong end of the stick will almost certainly jump into our hands. And in the case of stones, well, they can be approached from the wrong angle too. But never mind. There are links and connections. And not only between Pet Rocks and Crystals! And though the wrong end of the stick is invariably connected to the right end, it is an extremely long stick. Even longer than this metaphor.

So there we have it. That's what stones are all about. Questions. And while this may not be a very satisfying conclusion to those for whom answers are more interesting than questions, that's just the way it is. There are any number of answers for those who wish to be given them, any number of guides. Mostly completely unreliable. Psychics, cranks and renegade archaeologists will rush into print at the glow of a word processor and give the hopeful enquirer any number of answers. Those truly wishing to get to grips with the magic, ritual and religion of the ancients will make their own enquiry. Though as a leading psychic, crank and renegade archaeologist, this writer will offer one bit of advice. This advice is in the form of a question, naturally. What are the spaces *between* the stones in a stone circle for ?

STRING

Up to recently there were, at certain locations, pieces of string attached to stones which, correctly utilised, would provide relief from various ailments. Here we have connection to the practice of Celtic witches of breathing on string to which they had tied ritual knots. With correct incantations (send £500 to author) this would have a strong effect, usually though not exclusively, malevolent. String magic was widespread in witchcraft, even beyond the Celtic world, as evidenced by a prayer in the Koran for delivery from 'the mischief of women blowing on knots'.

T

TARBHFHEIS

'The Bull Feast' was a ritual carried out especially when a new King was to be chosen. A bull would be slaughtered, its flesh and blood eaten of by a druid, who would then go to sleep wrapped in its hide. There he would dream the name of the correct King. This ritual is also connected to the pagan custom of burial in a bull's hide and is certainly the historic root of activities carried out up to the last century. Then, when an individual was ill a sheep would be slaughtered and skinned. The patient would be wrapped in the skin while in a ritual circle around the friends and neighbours would consume the meat with suitable reverence.

Modern man would probably prefer to go to a hospital than be wrapped in the skin of a newly slaughtered sheep but this is a preference rather than a proof of efficiency. Ritual food, drink and meals, on a day-to-day level, are accepted without question by our culture. From naff wedding feasts of prawn cocktail, champagne and fruit cake, through business lunches, suburban sunday dinners, curry 'n chips at closing time, right on up the scale to unleavened bread at Church services, our food and drink is heavily ritualised. A bag of chips would not be an auspicious start to a business relationship. A thin-lipped emissary from Rome would soon arrive on the doorstep of any Catholic church that started services using fruit cake and champagne. We step out of line at our peril on these things. Literally we cannot survive unless we abide by the established ritual. We will lose our jobs, friends, family and the support of religion. Our possessions will be in a supermarket trolley. And our home a cardboard box. But. . . we should not despair. As the Supermarket-Trolley-Cardboard-Box Culture grows, so will an allied ritual. In the distant future the leaders of this culture may very well demand to be buried in large cardboard boxes. With 'Kelloggs' stamped on them. No-one will by then know what 'Kelloggs' means. . . except that it is always stamped on leaders' burial boxes!

THREE COINS IN A FOUNTAIN

A pleasant tune, a light-hearted film, and a Celtic custom of great antiquity; throwing coins into water is a remnant of ancient ritual. In actuality it appears that formerly the custom was to throw 'metal' into wells. Pins and suchlike predominated in offerings. Metal coins gradually came into use and, over time, the value of the offering was considered to be that of the currency rather than the actual metal. In modern urban Ireland shopping centre pools and ponds in public plazas are littered with coins. These are collected by organised charities or disorganised gangs of gougers. The people who throw in the coins do so, they would say, for 'luck'. Activities done for 'luck' in modern societies are remnants of ritual done at one time for survival.

TREES

The three trees held in special regard were Yew, Hawthorn and Rowan. The Yew was used for ritual inscriptions *(see page 104)*. The Hawthorn was sacred to the Tuatha dé Danaaan and is the 'fairy tree' of later folklore. (To this day no right-thinking person would bring a branch of this tree into their house !). The Rowan is mentioned in mythology as having the power of enchantment, its qualities are vague and mystical. The Oak, said to have been sacred to the Euro-Druids, has not been regarded as particularly important in Ireland though it was very prevalent and features in many place names. (Derry, for example, means 'oak wood'). The connection of pigs to oaks via their love of acorns is perhaps more important than the tree itself.

All cultures had sacred trees or 'Trees of Life'. In Germany to this day they 'marry' certain trees to each other by tying them together with rope. Which is perhaps connected to the old Irish expression, "a woman, a dog, and a walnut tree, the better you whip them, the better they be".

TROUSERS AND THE GODDESS

In ancient Ireland only the males of the lower orders wore trousers; warriors and aristocrats wore what were, in effect, skirts or dresses. This observation may seem superficial but such customs have origins that reveal deeper insights. In this instance it is a reminder of the connection between warrior and 'priest' in ancient systems, and a reminder that priests of all cultures invariably adopt female attire. This is because, in their function, they are descended from priestesses.

At the very begining the Gods were female and their priestesses like-wise. Modern male transvestites may very well be driven by some stray inherited characteristic connected to all this. It is interesting to note that the majority of such transvestites appear to want to perform functions related to *female public sexuality,* to coin a phrase. Rather than getting themselves up as housekeepers or child minders, other 'traditional' female functions, or indeed even as female executives or professionals, the modern tranvestites attire themselves as prostitutes, dancers, strippers or whatever.

A toe into the water of delicate feminist sensibilities here. The fact is that the ancient priestesses did use these activities in the service of the Goddess. Modern feminists make much of *the* Goddess. Unfortunately in their version she is more of an emanation of the American West Coast media than of the psychic core of our being. The *real* Goddess from time immemorial has been celebrated by either prostitute-priestesses or virgin-priestesses. The difference between prostitute and virgin in this case is, in liturgical terms, merely a modest technical difference similar to such as might arise between Methodist and Presbyterian. It really is. The fact is that female sexuality was considered the *essential* in the service of the Goddess. The fact that prostitution in our culture is sordid, dangerous and demeaning to the individual is no reason to believe that this must always be the case. Without comment we can merely note that a particular Christian cult in modern America sends its womenfolk out, as prostitutes, to recruit members. And one of the modern world's most successful female singers, generally attired as a tart, has adapted the appelation of Christianity's most sacred woman. There is no such thing as coincidence or accident; merely occurences to which we are unable to supply connections.

V

VATIS

These were a class of druid concerned with sacrifice and nature study. In Celtic life generally the three classes were Druids, Vatis, and Bards. Bards were occupied with the composition and chanting of ritual verse. In Ireland the classes were druids, filidh, and bards. Filidh and Vatis have semantic connections and thus we may safely infer that our filidh (regarded now as 'poets') were in fact concerned with more substantial matters.

W

WATER

Ireland does not ever appear to have been short of water. However, whether in surplus or not, water is perceived as the source of life and as such enjoys veneration and inspires mystery and awe in all societies. Modern man reacts particularly strongly to the pollution of water, of sea, or lake, or river. We put up with filthy air and desecrated landscape. . . what really offends is contaminated water. We will kill for clean water. Eventually, of course, we will have to kill off our present society to obtain clean water. . . but that lies a little in the future.

In the distant past the cultural roots of Ireland lay in countries where water was not in abundance. In those areas water has been given even more importance in the sense that the actual locations of water take on added significance. From this culture developed the notion that rivers are sacred to the point of being divine beings, lakes are personages, and wells are 'holy'. Not for a long time have we regarded our rivers and lakes as anything special, but the wells remain 'holy' to this day. Christian pilgrimages take place to the wells on particular days, usually associated with a saint, but these pilgrimages are merely successors or continuations of ancient customs. Apart from pilgrimages, wells are visited throughout the year for purposes associated with healing, some wells being good for particular ailments, and others associated with others. What all this means is . . . well . . .

WHIPS

A ritual performed by ancients was carried out thus. A ring of bare backed people sat, forming themselves into a circle. One person wandered around on the outside with a whip. The sitting people passed secretly, one to the other, a small stone or bead. The person outside the circle would suddenly ask an individual to say who had the pebble. A wrong answer brought a whipping but the whipped would then take over the role of the inquirer who would sit down with the rest. This went on until every individual had been whipped by every other. In more modern times variations on this custom persist in mystical flaggelation rituals.

WHITE MARES

A potential male ruler underwent a ceremony in which he 'married' Sovereignty, *(see page 80)*. A 'female' principle, sovereignty was represented at the ceremony by a white mare which was sacrificed and eaten. There is a connection here to the City of Armagh which takes its name from the mythological character Macha. A queen, she would manifest herself in the guise of a horse, taunting potential lovers/rulers with her speed. Macha has connections with the Welsh Rhiannon and the European Goddess Epona. Known as the 'Horse Goddess', Epona was actually a Goddess of land and of nature.

WISH BONE

Modern poultry eaters practise a little custom with this particular part of the bird; the origins of this lie in the habit of the ancients in examining the skeletons of birds for portents.

WITCH

A woman wishing to acquire the basic powers of witchcraft should perform the following ritual. Gather five oval and two flat stones, somewhat the size of a fist. Travel, with a selected companion (and the stones) to one of certain specified places around Ireland. Remove one's clothes. At midnight turn three times 'against the sun'. Essentially this means revolving anti-clockwise, a method of stirring up certain classes of spiritual entities. Lie on the ground, face up, head to the north, arms and legs out like the spokes of a wheel. An oval stone is placed, by the companion, at each foot, each hand, and between the legs. One of the flat stones is placed over the heart, tucked beneath the breast. The other flat stone is placed over the right breast. Thus read-ied, the witch-to-be will call upon the spirit of the place to give her power - in return she pledges herself to that particular spirit. She rises by rolling onto all fours to the left. Like this she travels animal-like in three circles, returning then to the scattered seven stones. She casts one of these away. Then three more animal-like circles, all anti-clockwise, back to the stones, casts another away. She repeats this until all stones are dispersed and then rises to her feet, puts on her clothes, and goes about her business. Though apparently farcial, none of this should be taken lightly. (To avoid a plague of witches this writer has omitted the 'certain specified places'). The interesting thing about this ritual, which is of late date, is the connection it draws between stone, woman, and particular place. These are three of the fundamentals of the ancient psychic system.

WORDSWORTH

William Wordsworth is understood by many to have been a goofey English poet who may have had an unnatural relationship with his sister but. . .he is important as a representative of modern pantheism, or 'seeing God in everything'. Up to very recently this was regarded as totally unChristian (which of course it is!) but with the rise of New Age concepts Christianity has adjusted and is itself starting to 'see God in everything'.

People were burnt at the stake for this in earlier Christian ages but those times of certainty have been replaced by the Age of Chaos. Here, where we live now, our beliefs are merely attempts to come to terms with this chaos rather that efforts to relate to the Truth. Each day we see the world differently. Chaos escalates and yesterday's beliefs rapidly become 'irrelevant'. Mankind has a great fear of 'irrelevance'. This fear has replaced the traditional fear of hell. Hell for a modern opinion former is, in fact, a place where one is never interviewed. And Heaven is existence under a constant barrage of media attention. No matter the content of your views or the veracity of your beliefs. You can be completely deranged and still 'relevant'. In fact, the more deranged, the more 'relevant'. Serial killers who boil human heads on their cooker are more or less at the pinnacle of this relevance. Behind them in the league come ordinary criminals and psychotics, followed by pop singers, business leaders, women-with-big-breasts and, bringing up the rear, Christian bishops. However, a Bishop who runs away with a woman-with-big-breasts or, for that matter, boils her head on his cooker, he immediately shoots to the top position in the scale of 'relevance'. Such is the Age of Chaos where we 'see God in everything'.

And the connection between this and the magic, ritual and religion of the ancients ? Very close. Our Age of Chaos is an interim stage. 'Seeing God in everything' is a temporary philosophic position. After a while it will be realised that 'everything' contains so many contradictions and alternatives that, far from being a 'wholeness', it is a construct of antagonistic forces held in balance. The forces are seen as 'good', 'bad', 'light', 'dark', 'ying' or 'yang' or whatever. The names are irrelevant. Attempts to make society totally 'good' ot totally 'bad' are equally doomed. The natural state is a balance between these forces; these different spirit entities, psychic movements, Gods or Goddesses or whatever. 'Seeing God in everything' leads inevitably to 'seeing- Gods and Goddesses in everything'. Thus is the all-powerful God of our Christian culture splitting up into a myriad different Gods and Goddesses, some good, some mediocre, and some particularly nasty bits of work. To rise up out of our Age of Chaos, to restore a balance, it is necessary to recognise all of these, and to behave towards each in the appropriate manner. This is why folks read books like the present one. They are searching for systems, answers, secrets. Francis of Assissi put it well. "The one you are looking for is the one who is looking".

WORSAAE

A Danish antiquarian who in 1819, with his colleague Thomsen, suggested that history stretched far further back than then generally accepted. Up to then mankind was believed to have started up around 5000BC, it having being precisely calculated that God created Man at 9 o'clock in the morning of October the twenty-third, 4000BC. Even such noted scholars as Isaac Newton found it impossible to accept that Egyptian mummies might be dated to 5000BC. We now know that man was around 40,000 years ago and that, in the few thousand years BC where lie the roots of early Ireland, man had wheeled vehicles, advanced agriculture, painting, weaving, pottery and metals.

XYZ

X

The shape of 'Saint Brigid's Cross' is actually that of an 'X'. This is the shape of the spokes of a wheel and an ancient symbol of the sun, rolling round the heavens.

YEW STICKS

Wands or sticks of this tree were cast by Irish magicians to foretell the future. The Magi of the East threw little sticks of tamarisk wood for the

the same purpose. The links between the two cultures are perhaps via the Tuatha dé Danaan and Finland. From the 'northern islands', the dé Danaan brought to Ireland the magical arts. The magic/mythology of pagan Finland has very strong connections with that of ancient Chaldean civilizations. In Wales the magicians used 'Coelbreni', translated as 'omen-sticks'. There the fires lit at Samhain were known as coel-coeth, omen-fires. Coelcannon is a modern cabbage dish eaten particularly at Hallowe'en, which is Samhain. While all these links may not be obvious, they are certainly there.

ZODIAC

The representation of figures in the Irish Zodiac were distinct; the figure of Sagittarius was a deer's body with a man's head; Libra had legs, but no feet; Virgo was a standing fully-clothed figure wearing shoes and shown spinning; Aquarius had a very long body with very short thin legs and little feet.

111

MINI BIBLIOGRAPHY

General 'Ancient Ireland' interest:

Shell Guide to Ireland *(Dublin 1989)*, Duignan/Morris/Harbison.

Archaeological Interest:

National & Historic Monuments of Ireland
(Dublin1992) Harbison.

Ancient Monuments - Sacred Sites
(1998, FACT PACK*)* Kennedy.

Mythological Interest:

Guide to Irish Mythology *(Dublin 1996)* D.Smyth.

Places of Mythology *(1998,* FACT PACK*)* Kennedy & Smyth.

Dictionary of Irish Mythology (London 1988) Berresford-Ellis.

*FACT PACK titles are published by Morrigan Books, Killala, Co Mayo, Ireland.

website
http:// www.atlanticisland.ie